Scrying the Secrets

of the Future

How to Use

Crystal Balls,

Fire, Wax, Mirrors,

Shadows, and

Spirit Guides to

Reveal Your Destiny

Cassandra
Eason

This edition first published in 2007 by New Page Books, an imprint of
Red Wheel/Weiser, LLC
With offices at:
65 Parker Street, Suite 7
Newburyport, MA 01950
www.redwheelweiser.com
www.newpagebooks.com

ISBN: 978-1-56414-908-4
Library of Congress Cataloging-in-Publication Data
Eason, Cassandra.
    Scrying the secrets of the future : how to use crystal balls,
water, fire, wax, mirrors, shadows, and spirit guides to reveal your
destiny / by Cassandra Eason.
        p. cm.
    Includes index.
    ISBN-13: 978-1-56414-908-4
    ISBN-10: 1-56414-908-0
    1. Crystal gazing. 2. Divination. I. Title.
BF1335.E24 2007
133.--dc22

2006030546

Cover design by Jean William Naumann
Interior by Gina Talucci

Printed in the United States of America
IBI
10 9 8 7 6 5 4 3 2 1

Contents

Introduction   5

Chapter 1: How Scrying Works   11

Chapter 2: Preparations for Scrying   23

Chapter 3: Scrying With Water   45

Chapter 4: Scrying With Fire   65

Chapter 5: Scrying With Air   87

Chapter 6: Earth Scrying   107

Chapter 7: Scrying With Wax   121

Chapter 8: Ink and Oil Scrying   137

Chapter 9: Dream Scrying   153

Chapter 10: Scrying With Mirrors   163

Chapter 11: Dark Mirror Scrying   183

Chapter 12: Scrying With Crystal Balls   201

Chapter 13: Scrying With Tea Leaves
    and Coffee Grounds   219

Chapter 14: Scrying With Shadows   239

Appendix: The Deities of Fate   259

Useful Reading   263

Index   267

About the Author   271

Introduction

Scrying is an old word, rooted in the Anglo-Saxons and means *to perceive dimly* or *to reveal*. Scrying is an ancient art that involves gazing into reflective surfaces such as water, a mirror, or shimmering flames. Within them, the scryer can see information unknown by the conscious mind in the present time.

Scrying was probably practiced long before written records show, as our distant ancestors gazed into pools by moonlight, looked into the fire, or observed recognizable shapes of people or animals in the clouds. The early scryers, similar to modern-day ones, saw pictures that were not physically present but that appeared as physical images on the surface of, or within the scrying medium. These images sometimes revealed, through symbols, actual scenes from the future and possible opportunities for the scryer. I have written more about symbols, the key to scrying, later in the book.

People have always wanted to know what the future holds, whether they are on the right track, and about the health and safety of loved ones, especially family members. In pretelecommunication days, family members might be away for long periods of time and unable to send news.

Therefore, scrying has always been a very personal art, practiced by ordinary people in their homes with ordinary pots and pans, as well as by priests, priestesses, Witches, and magicians who scryed in sacred vessels.

The Secrets of Scrying

What we observe while scrying into water or crystals is often hazy or fleeting because we are not observing rock solid, here-and-now events, but a future with many uncertainties and choices, influenced partly by the future actions of those around us and more global forces beyond our control.

But with practice and effort we can bring that unstable future into sharp focus so that we can study the options ahead and shape our actions to influence or change our potential destiny.

Aristotle, the Greek philosopher, described water scrying in his *Prophesying by Dreams* in 350 b.c.: "If the motion in the water be great, the reflection has no resemblance to its original, nor do the forms resemble the real objects." If this were true, he was probably skillful at interpreting such reflections, which he could rapidly discern, and at a glance comprehend, the scattered and distorted fragments of such forms. And skilful we can become in scrying in a remarkably short time.

Srying in the Modern Word

Scrying in order to discover future opportunities and hazards is even more essential in the modern world, where too often we have been taught to distrust our guiding intuitions and protective psychic radar.

Scrying is a necessary step in checking within ourselves for our dreams. Often, we know the right answers as to what is right for us, and where, how, with whom, and on what terms we would prefer to live.

Scrying also connects us with the Universal Web or Well of Wisdom or, as the psychologist Carl Jung called it, the Collective Unconscious. Another term for this cosmic memory bank is the Akashic Records. This universal treasury contains the knowledge and experiences of all people and places in all times and the potential of the future.

The limitations of measured or clock time do not apply once we reach this deeper level of wisdom, and so we can step outside the restrictions of this being 3 p.m. on August 30th in the UK where I am writing. Of course the same moment is actually 4 p.m. in Scandinavia and 7 a.m. in Los Angeles! More on this later in the book.

Often in scrying, we can receive messages through symbols from our Guardian Angel, our Spirit Guides, and our own wise evolved spiritual self—the part of us that may survive death and that works to make life and the world better.

Clairvoyance, Scrying, and Psychic Powers

The ability to scry is rooted in the power called clairvoyance. Clairvoyance, or *clear seeing*, means scrying with a crystal sphere, a bowl of water, or whatever you choose to work with. As a result, the scryer will see psychically induced images that, once interpreted, hold the answer to the question you asked or the dominant issue in your life you were thinking about when you began the scrying.

The images are projected by the inner or psychic eye into your chosen scrying tool, so that you can physically see them, even though some images may be symbolic, holding a lot of extra information you need to decipher.

Clairvoyant vision, which is central to scrying, is not restricted by the limits of the physical eye range. Clairvoyance also enables us to look into past worlds and lives that hold clues to present dilemmas, as well as forwards to the future and other dimensions. We can, with practice, *see* those other worlds in the water or crystal. Though there have been and still are numerous experiments in parapsychology and clairvoyance on both sides of the Atlantic, scrying tends not to be a sufficiently precise art amenable to measurements or modern computer techniques. The exception is remote viewing, the ability to see events beyond the physical eye range or events hidden within opaque containers. Many of the experiments are carried out in the field. Though the seeker does not use a scrying medium as such, the art is closely related to scrying.

When we scry, we can see distant people, places, or beings from other dimensions by a process called remote viewing. The term *remote viewing* was first used by Russell Targ and Harold Puthoff. After hundreds of experiments for more than 10 years at Stanford Research Institute International in California, these two researchers concluded that remote viewing is a psychic power that many people experience spontaneously. The researchers found that subjects who had little previous psychic experience could be taught quite rapidly to accurately describe buildings, geographic features, people, and activities in distant locations. People were also taught to see and describe the contents of opaque containers (the scrying connection).

Also with practice, we can connect and communicate with spiritual beings who belong to those dimensions, including an-gels, nature essences, Spirit Guides, and wise ancestors who have chosen to act as teachers. These may be actual ancestors from way back in our past or ones from other cultures to whom we are spiritually linked.

Scrying may also bring messages, signs, and even glimpses of our own deceased family. All these can be perceived through the art of scrying and can be learned by anyone.

But What Do These Images Mean?

Clairvoyance incorporates other innate psychic powers that are activated by the scrying process. These extra psychic senses explain and expand through words, internal images in our mind, and feelings. These additional powers enable us to apply their significance to the questions we are asking, using our normal analytical processes, enhanced by a new intuitive awareness of what we cannot logically know. Scrying is essentially a multisensory experience.

These psychic powers include clairaudience, the ability to hear with your inner psychic ear. These words are filtered from your own deep, often inaccessible knowledge, from the Collective Unconscious, Spirit Guides, Angels, and even the voice of a wise departed grandmother that reminds us, or the client through us, of a forgotten childhood memory. Such words help to verify the experience, especially when connecting with the deceased. Often, however, the words will be spoken internally by your normal inner voice.

Clairsentience, or psychic sensing, enhanced by burning fragrances, such as oils, incense, or scented candles while scrying, manifests into impressions in our mind that help us to tune into what we *feel* about an image or symbol we have seen clairvoyantly. For scrying, this is the most vital psychic sense of all. If, for example, there was a half-open door seen in a crystal ball, is it conveying hope of an opportunity previously closed or suggesting a door should be closed? This subtle sense is valuable in fine-tuning initial impressions and in helping you to know instinctively what the door is saying about your best course for the future.

Divination and Scrying

Divination means consulting the wise divus or diva, God or Goddess, Divine energy source, and different deities of fate that have been consulted throughout time, as I will describe in the next chapter.

In the modern world we may find such ideas strange, but the principle is the same. What you are doing when you scry is what our ancestors did, but they attributed all the knowledge to an external divine source, rather than their own evolved inner wisdom (plus the intervention of Guardian Angels and so on).

You may find it easier to work with the concept of the divus or diva that exists within us all. Every one of us has a wise, evolved inner spirit or Divine spark that remindes us we are spiritual beings in a physical body and not the other way around.

Scrying is a major form of divination, though often the term *divination* is used to refer to more structured methods of clair-voyance, such as Tarot. In this book, I use the terms *scrying* and *divination* interchangeably.

Chapter 1

How Scrying Works

Scrying is a natural process that draws on the vast, untapped resources of the human mind. It is not intended to replace logic, analysis, or the reasoning processes of everyday thinking. Rather, it supplements what we *see* as already known with unknown or unprocessed information. Scrying also offers a dynamic, creative way of making connections between apparently unrelated factors.

Central to scrying is the interpretation of symbols that appear in or on the surface of the scrying medium (for example, formed by floating ink on water).

Symbols, according to 20th-century occultist Dion Fortune, are believed to contain the energies and experiences of all the people who had used them or seen the actual manifestation of the symbol in real life.

Processing Psychic Information

The right side of the brain, from which the imagination comes, is the hemisphere through which clairvoyance and scrying abilities may be most readily developed. With this often under-utilized hemisphere, we can anticipate with great accuracy a future not yet made, recall verifiable details of a past we did not consciously experience, and derive images or actual scenes about people and places currently beyond the physical eye range.

The right hemisphere can effectively manipulate these images and also deal with hypotheses of future events without needing facts and figures.

The left side of the brain is more concerned with organizing present experiences and our consciously recalled past. In daily life, this is the vital part of the brain that enables us to function within measured time and recall useful facts from our past. The behavior, experiences, and relationships from our past guide us to make sensible choices or steer us away from hazards; it works mainly in words.

Of course predictions of the future can be made from what is already known and by assessing likeness. But when we add our imaginative powers to the right brain, to the deducing process of the left brain, we can bring to the fore what is not expected or reasonably predictable—and use these prophecies to make sensible choices in the here and now.

The previously mentioned is of course, a simplification, and you may wish to study detailed accounts of recent and past experiments in parapsychology.

This unknown information can also be given in the images we see during scrying by our Spirit Guides, angels, and recently deceased family members or spiritual ancestors.

If you are relatively new to the art you may have to prompt yourself at first: *What do I feel about this image, as I hold the crystal ball? What extra information comes through my fingertips, and what is the message I hear about the scrying experience?*

But eventually, as soon as you see a picture in your crystal or mirror, your mind will be flooded with words and impressions, and your fingertips may actually tingle.

What Is Time in the Scrying World?

In scrying, clock time is relative. Early moon calendars were an accurate way of predicting the migration or return of certain birds, or the arrival of the herds that occurred regularly after a set number of full moons.

However, lunar calendars were at odds with dates calculated by the sun. The Celtic Coligny calendar, for example, inserted an extra month called Ciallos every two and a half to three years. Ciallos was the month of no time, meant to synchronize with the sun's path through the skies

But solar time, as calculated by the apparent movement of the sun through the skies, has flaws of its own. We compensate for these with leap years.

Because the length of the day according to solar time is not the same throughout the year, calculated solar time was invented, based on the motion of a hypothetical sun traveling at an even rate throughout the year. The difference in the length of a 24-hour day at different seasons of the year can be as much as 16 minutes.

Standard time, which is based on solar time, was introduced in 1883, and the Earth was officially divided into 24 time zones.

The base position is the zero meridian of longitude that passes through the Royal Greenwich Observatory, Greenwich, England, and time zones are described by their distance east or west of Greenwich. Within each time zone, all clocks are set to the same time. In 1966, the U.S. Congress passed the Uniform Time Act, which established eight standard time zones for the United States. In 1983, several time zone boundaries were altered so that Alaska, which had formerly spanned four zones, could be nearly unified.

Turning Back the Clock

Take a bowl of water and look into it, recalling a momentous day in your past: the day you earned your first paycheck, your wedding day, the day you had your first child. Relive every moment as you look into the water: words, feelings, fragrances, and tastes, and, above all, look through the eyes of the person you were then.

Close your eyes and you may see the scene within the water as if you were looking down at it, yet it is still in your mind. Most of us cry when we recall losing someone we love, even 10 or 20 years later. Now go forward and anticipate getting off the plane on a trip you have saved all year for, especially if it is a place you love and have visited before. Live the moment fully—what you will feel and say, or the smell of the brewing coffee or the orange groves after rain. Both moments were real, and both were beyond measured time that has been ticking away while you walked down memory lane and explored tomorrow.

Back to the Future

You can also scry to discover a time frame within which a prediction will occur. How long before I meet my life partner, become pregnant, or get the job offer I am working towards? You can see ahead in pictures or symbols in the water. But when? A month, a year, or further away? If you want to know more precisely, focus on your image in the water and look for clues.

In the water, or in you mind, picture yourself and add the backcloth. Do you look older? How much older? Is it fall or spring? Can you see any clues—for example, your brother's presence when you know he is coming home for a holiday in six months? Does it feel soon? If you don't see the image you expected, work with what you do see, no matter what it is.

Working With Symbols

Children work with pictures rather than words when they are young. Jane, age 4, asked her mother Suzie if Aunty Anne would be taking care of her when her mother went out for the evening. Asked how Jane could know she was hoping to go out, because at the time no plans had been made, Jane said, "I can see you in your blue dress, with your new lipstick on."

"Where can you see me?" asked Suzie.

"In your mind, of course," replied Jane. "I can see the picture in your mind."

Five minutes before, Suzie had been day dreaming of getting ready and putting on her new blue dress to go out, and Jane had been sitting with her and watching.

As adults we tend to be much more word-based, but we still retain deep inside us, underneath the categories and the rationalizations and the neat boxes in which we file experiences, that natural clairvoyance and ease with symbols children take for granted, especially if we slow down and sit still as young Jane did.

Interpreting Symbols

To begin understanding symbols, let's use the example of a flower seen in oils floated on water, when Olivia asked the question of whether there was anyone out there that cared about her after 20 years of marriage.

Pretend you are trying to interpret the flower. The flower outline acts as a key to the inner vision of an actual flower, or one from the astral or spiritual plane. Flowers signify love, gifts, growth, and beauty. Now probe further to understand the deeper meaning of the specific flower shown.

For example, observe if the flower is blooming, budding, starting to wilt, or dying. Where is the flower? Is it in its natural place, growing in the ground, or has it been cut? Cut flowers give pleasure and may signify a celebration, either as part of a bouquet or a single rose given in love. But cut flowers do quickly lose their vitality and will not grow for much longer.

Is the flower being given as a peace offering, received with love, rejected, an exhibit in a flower show winning a prize? Has it been tossed on the ground or trampled underfoot, cast into water as an offering, or worn in the hair? Is it a tall graceful flower in a vase, a small wildflower in a meadow, or a well-tended flower in a neat flowerbed? What color is it—brilliant and tropical, or pale and delicate? What do you feel about the flower image? Do you pick up feelings of love at the gift, or sadness because it is dying or abandoned? Is it fragrant or just a decorative silk or paper flower? If it is not a real flower, what is not real about your present situation or relationship? What words or phrases do you hear in your mind? Is the flower a kind that was loved by a deceased relative you have been trying to contact, and so carries a message from that loved one? Is it offered to you by someone living but who is far away and thinking of you? What does the flower say to you and about the situation you are thinking of right now?

You can then apply all the information that has been gained from the single outline of the flower to the real-life situation. In fact, Olivia said the flower was in a weed patch, dying, but she believed it was still alive. Olivia said the weeds would need to be cleared away by her husband who worked 24/7 and only spoke to her when he wanted sex or a clean shirt. But she still believed the relationship was worth some effort and one last chance.

The more you develop your clairvoyant powers, the more your visions will appear as symbols, because symbols contain information that is far deeper and more spiritual than a straightforward representation of a scene.

The Powers Involved in Scrying and How to Develop Them

Clairvoyance

Clairvoyance, in the sense of clear seeing as opposed to the umbrella term that incorporates all the psychic senses, first involves seeing a physical image within the scrying medium. Then the scryer makes that image come to life either within the water, mirror, or on the inner screen within their mind. It is easier to animate an image in some scrying tools than others.

Crystal balls and water are best for revealing physically moving detailed images, whereas coffee grounds or candle wax may trigger stronger inner clairvoyant images. It really depends on the individual.

The following technique, called eidetic imagery, is one I teach to new clairvoyants and also more experienced ones who feel blocked. Start by looking at a large detailed picture or photograph, preferably brightly colored. Study it for a few minutes, either on a plain table with a white cloth or hung on a plain wall. Memorize every detail. Next, take the picture away and stare at the surface of the wall or table and imagine the picture still being there, building up the details from the center, persevering until you can project every detail on the wall.

Now, look out of the window at a familiar scene and memorize the details of that, noting anything unusual such as a strange cat sitting in the middle of the grass. When you have committed the image to memory, turn around and project it on the wall, this time not consciously inserting details, but allowing them to emerge slowly on their own.

Finally, picture a scene from the past where you were happy and, in your mind, paint it on the wall. We will work further with this technique in Chapter 10.

Clairaudience

Clairaudience is primarily the ability to hear words or sounds that are not part of the material world, which may be wisdom channeled from wise Spirit Guides, nature essences, or the devas, the higher nature spirits akin to angels (especially when scrying outdoors). You may also receive messages from angels, ancestors, and deceased loved ones externally or more frequently with clairaudience in your mind.

As you become more clairaudient, you will be able to distinguish your own wise inner voice from the background noise we all carry in our heads, whether as free-floating worries or lists of jobs to be finished.

Developing Your Psychic Ear and Voice

The development of clairaudience also enables us to speak wisely and with kindness if we are reading for others. It helps us to speak spontaneously about what will be helpful, and to remain silent about something we have seen that the other person may not be ready to accept or that would detract from the main positive message.

Such words that seem not to be ours, though spoken in our voice to a client or friend, can be very healing and empowering. They can lift what may be an accurate reading into one that inspires and points to a new window of opportunity in a situation that previously seemed closed or hopeless.

Tuning Into Psychic Sounds

To strengthen your innate clairaudient abilities, listen to sounds people have heard in other times and places, so your psychic ear becomes aware through the sounds of those other times and dimensions. The sounds may trigger images, fragrances, tastes, impressions, or scenes of occasions when bells called people to church for a wedding or a Sunday service. For places with good sounds you can try:

- ✎ Stand in a crowded market, close your eyes, and let the calls of the vendors carry you to earlier markets and fairs. At Christmas and special occasions, the old trades may be revived and, with them, the smells as well as the sounds of past centuries.

- ✎ Church, cathedral, or temple bells ringing out in celebration and calling the faithful to worship.

- ✎ A choir singing in Latin or another language you do not know, preferably heard in a high-vaulted cathedral or abbey. Buy a CD so you can listen at home or in the car.

- ✎ Ships at a port and vendors selling fish on the beach.

- ✎ Bird song, if possible in natural surroundings, both in the day and as they fly around before nesting at night. The call of seagulls can be especially evocative.

- ✎ Farm animals, especially when they have their young and are calling to them; also free-running hens and cockerels.

- ✎ Children playing.

When you are confident, you can try without the physical sound stimuli, choosing instead a location that will have absorbed sounds into the walls or stones through the centuries; old places hold the sounds of the past in their walls. People have reported hearing church bells under lakes, only to learn later of legends of sunken villages beneath the water.

It may be possible to do detective work in a local museum or library to understand the context of a seemingly unrelated sound. For example, in Cornwall in South West England on Bodmin Moor there are disused tin mines. Echoes of this once, thriving industry can be heard on misty evenings and at dawn when the shifts would have started or ended.

Clairsentience and Psychometry

These two psychic senses are very close and can be practiced through the same exercise. Clairsentience, as I have already mentioned, is vital as a guide to what you feel about an image.

Incenses, oils, and scented candles are very powerful triggers of clairsentient abilities and make it possible for you to move into a light trance state or higher level of awareness where hidden knowledge becomes accessible during scrying.

Psychometry, the art of psychic touch, operates through the sensitive chakras in the palms of the hands and fingertips that respectively link with the green Heart chakra energy center.

Psychic touch operates as a transmitter of our personal psychic energies, so when you or a client holds a crystal ball, it will enable you to pick up psychic impressions about the other person. More importantly, your crystal, mirror, and any medium, such as a fire, have an aura or energy field in the same way humans do. Psychic information that will help you tune into your scrying will be activated through your fingertips.

Clairsentience, Psychometry, and Old Places

Choose a location that is, if possible, at least 100 years of history, and with which you are not familiar. Perhaps a reconstructed Gold Rush outpost, an industrial museum where there are original artifacts, or a haunted house would suffice. Gettysburg, Salem, or the Plymouth area where the Pilgrim Fathers landed, the Serpent Mound in Ohio, the Heights of Abraham in Quebec, or a historical city such as Boston are ideal, because there were so many powerful events there. Museums where you can handle artifacts will give you a wide range of cultures, one of which you may have an affinity to.

Go to an established forest, perhaps connected with an indigenous culture, or to a botanical garden where there will be Nature devas, spirits, and fragrances, such as rose or lavender, to carry you to other times. The best times to visit are in the morning or evening when it is quiet. Do not study the history in advance; avoid guided tours until you have formed your own impressions.

Close your eyes, use your fingertips and palms to make connection, and let the impressions flow. Afterward, check the accuracy of what you sensed of the people who lived there. If there is a pool, lake, or river, look into it with your eyes half-closed and let the images reflect perhaps another time when others once gazed into the water.

Dedicating Your Scrying to the Deities of Fate

Every culture has its deities of fate, usually three sisters who oversee the interweaving web of past, present, and future, or three Crones or wise Grandmother Goddesses. They were often were spinners or weavers of the web of human destiny and even that of the deities.

You can dedicate your scrying to any of them you feel akin to. I have listed angels and deities in the individual chapters (for example, Hathor for mirror scrying). Shadow and smoke scrying are often blessed by our personal Spirit Guides.

Each of the Fate Sister triplicates has their own candle color, incense, and crystal you can use as a focus when connecting with their energies. (For more information, see the Appendix.)

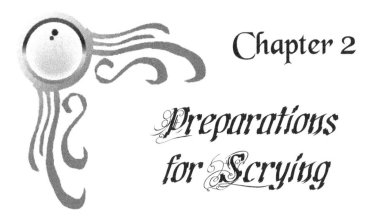

Chapter 2

Preparations for Scrying

The most memorable scrying experiences are usually spontaneous ones, such as when you find a small lake in the middle of the forest with a legend of a magical guardian and cast stones to make ripples. It may be when you have had a truly awful day and you look in the mirror of a garishly lit hotel bedroom. After weeks of trying to see images in vain, suddenly they are there rippling on the surface. Similar to the good fairy on your child's naming day, bubbling pictures appear in the suds of the washing bowl.

However, by making a special place in your home as well and collecting special crystals, fragrances, and bowls for your scrying work, even five or 10 minutes taken out of a busy day will make the occasion special and blessed. When you can spiritually and mentally put a distance between you and the everyday world, connecting with the world of images and hidden messages becomes so much easier.

Finally, basic psychic protection and closing down after scrying work ensures that you do not open yourself too much to the sorrows of others, or feel unable to switch off after focusing on spiritual realms. This is a very practical chapter.

Basic Materials for Scrying

To start off with, you will need sea salt, sage, rosemary, chives, tarragon, basil, bay leaves, dried lavender heads and rose petals, hyssop, mugwort, and pennyroyal. The last three are for making cleansing infusions and dark scrying waters, and can be obtained ready dried from herbal stores or online.

Next you will need candles in a variety of sizes and colors, where the color goes all the way through, not just on the surface, for wax scrying. You can use the cheaper dipped-colored candles for light and for gazing into the flame. Have some scented candles for working with other dimensions, especially floral fragrances that provide a gentle bridge of perfume to help connect with visions of angels and ancestors.

Keep a supply of different fragrant oils for hot oil scrying and a small bottle of dark high quality palm or virgin olive oil for cold scrying. Cheaper dark fragrance oils are also good for floating on cold water to make images.

A Scrying Place

A small, private place indoors where you can keep your scrying materials and work undisturbed rapidly becomes a center of peace and sanctity in your home. There is no harm in others touching your things but, as a mother of five, I did not establish enough boundaries in the early days. My precious things were often scattered and my peace disturbed.

If you do live in a busy household you need a quiet corner. Clear out a cluttered attic, erect a chalet, or make a screened-off area, with boxes for your scrying tools and materials when not in use. Your space is as important as your partner's den, the children's TV room, and the sacrosanct spare room that may be empty half the year.

Just spending five or 10 minutes every day looking into your crystal ball by candlelight will build up your own still spiritual center even more than formal exercises, and put the world into perspective.

What You Will Need

- A table large enough to hold your equipment so that you are not constantly shuffling things around or searching for what you need, especially if you are carrying out clairvoyance for others.

- A cloth that you can change according to your own preferences.

- Soft lighting. Candles are not only valuable scrying tools but, when lit after dark, they create an enclosed center of light and sphere of protection.

- A central white or beeswax candle in the center of the table that you replace whenever it becomes worn down. At night add extra candles, if necessary, appropriate to the form of scrying.

- Incense in a holder on the right side of the table so you sit facing it. You can use incense sticks or cones, or, if you prefer, loose granular or powdered incense burned on a white hot charcoal disk. You can also use an oil fragrance burner, the kind with a bowl for the oil, which is heated by a small candle underneath. Carnation, frankincense, lavender, lily, myrrh, rose, pine, and sandalwood are some of the effective divinatory fragrances that relax the conscious mind.

- A smudge stick. This is a dried bundle of herbs, usually cedar or sage, that are tied together with thread. One end is lit and blown out so it glows red and smoke pours in a steady stream from the end. You hold the other end in your hand as it is quite cool. If you don't like smoke, keep fresh fragrant flowers on the table and move the incense or smudge off the table once you have used it to purify and empower your working area.

- A small dish of sea salt on the far side of the table as you face it. Keep this topped up and fresh.

- A small bowl of tap or still mineral water on the left of the table as you face it.

- A clear crystal pendulum that can be used for instantly empowering or cleansing divinatory tools or your sacred space. Keep the pendulum horizontally on the table in front of the candle nearest to you, when it is not in use.

- A hand bell, small Tibetan bell cymbals, a small singing bowl, a string of bells, or a rattle to cleanse and clear the space before and after scrying. This can go on the far side of your table as you sit facing it, if there is room.

- A clear crystal quartz point for making protective circles around yourself or your tools and directing light to cleanse an area. Keep this horizontally in front of the pendulum on your table.

- Your special tools and materials for your scrying and clairvoyant work (much more on these in later chapters). You can use any household bowls for scrying, however, use them for this purpose only.

You can pick up mirrors, candlesticks, and other useful artifacts from garage sales or market stalls, or ask older relatives, who may have materials stored away. I have listed the individual requirements in the separate chapters and also special ways of cleansing and empowering them before use.

Pride of place has to be your crystal ball that some people cover with a dark cloth when not in use. For scrying, set it either on a special stand or a dark piece of cloth to avoid reflections. If you leave it uncovered it spreads light and healing throughout the room and the home. I'll write more on choosing a ball in the chapter on crystal spheres, but I advise picking a crystal with cracks or inclusions inside the clear quartz.

Buy or make a large wooden box or chest in which you can keep your divinatory tools when not in use. You can also wrap them in cloth or individual bags made of natural fabric. Have a separate smaller box for oils, herbs, dried petals, candles, and incense. Keep supplies topped up regularly.

You can also make a small traveling bag containing a spare quartz pendulum, a small crystal ball, a small bell, a sage smudge stick, an additional crystal point, and a small bowl that you can take out into the garden or countryside for open air scrying.

Keeping a Scrying Journal

If you have a computer, you can keep an ongoing record that can be easily edited and categorized, but have a hand-written record of your scrying experiences Also, you can often buy plain paper notebooks with beautiful covers, and, where possible, you should write in it using proper pen and ink rather than a ballpoint pen. This journal will become a gift for future generations.

Record any channeled wisdom you receive from angels, Spirit Guides, or ancestors. Date any predictions you make for yourself or others and write down predictive or significant dreams, so you can monitor their accuracy. Note any details of angelic presences and past worlds you see during scrying, and you may be able to research these further.

Keep an ongoing alphabetic collection of personal symbol meanings. This will be based on your personal scrying and dreams, plus any myths or folklore you encounter that will enrich your understanding of individual symbols. Some scryers keep a special loose-leaf folder or online record for symbols so that they can add them to the symbol meanings as they encounter them. If you did that, you could then create a special summary section of the most important symbols (listed alphabetically) in your permanent journal.

If you do work professionally as a clairvoyant or medium and have regular clients, brief notes can help to take up where you left off and enquire about what has happened in their lives since the last consultation. If you do a number of readings, details can become blurred without notes. It is also courteous to note names of partners and children to avoid having to keep asking.

Make personal spiritual targets and goals for approximate time frames in the future.

Personal Preparations For Scrying

To completely cut out all personal spiritual preparation and protection is similar to driving without a seat belt. Most of the time you are okay, but there is a risk if things do go wrong. Psychic energies do need to be activated and then closed down after use, even with a brief word or two of blessing if time is at a premium.

Read the following section, choose your favorites, and adapt them for different needs and levels of work so that you develop your own routine. Note that you would not do all of them.

Preparing the Place

First make sure you have everything on the table that you are going to use. Then, ring your bell or rattle around the room to clear the space of stagnant energies (rattles work well outdoors, too). Alternatively, you can spiral your pendulum around the room in all directions, clockwise and counterclockwise, so the light catches it. Then, plunge it nine times into a glass of water that you throw away afterward. Nine is a magical number—the sacred three times three that indicates perfection and completion, and in this case complete cleansing.

Another method is to use a sage or cedar smudge stick or a large firm incense stick in pine, lemon, rosemary, juniper, or sage. Move it in a circular motion over the table and around the room and say, "Be purified and blessed and may only goodness and light enter here." You can use these words with the pendulum method as well.

Another method is to drop three pinches of salt from your salt bowl into the bowl of clear water on your table, stir it three times clockwise with your clear crystal point or the index finger of the hand you write with. Sprinkle the water around the room, then at each of the four corners of the table, and just one or two drops over the center of the table, saying the same words. If you are in a public place where you can't do anything openly, hold your crystal point in the hand you write with, facing outwards, and picture beams of light radiating from it, cleansing the space. You can say the words in your mind.

To strengthen any of the ways of protection, when you begin scrying and light your center candle, drop a pinch of salt from your salt bowl into the flame and repeat the protective words we just talked about in your mind.

Casting Further Protection Around Your Tools

Any of the previously mentioned methods will automatically protect and empower your tools. However, I have listed ways in each of the chapters that are most effective with the individual methods. When scrying outdoors with nature you need much less protection and can ask the devas, the higher guardians of the forest or lakeside, to bless and protect your work.

Clearing Your Personal Energy Field

When you do have time, try to slow your activities down in the hours before a scrying session, such as eating a light meal and turning your phone, faxes, and computers on silent at least half an hour before you begin. If you have time, prepare yourself with a warm bath or shower. Add three pinches of salt to the bath water or under the running shower and use a psychically cleansing bath or shower product in a pine, eucalyptus, lemon, tea tree, rose, rosemary, or lavender fragrance (or a mixture). If possible to do safely, light some scented candles in the bathroom so the light shines in the water

Wash your body downwards, in counterclockwise circles. Rinse your hair. If you are using a shower, rub an essential oil shower mix onto your body in the same way.

When you are ready to get out of the water, swirl the reflected light three times counterclockwise and take out the plug, visualizing any clutter from the day being washed away.

You can do this after you have turned off the shower as the water drains away. Blow out the candles and send the light into your energy field or aura unless you are using them for dream scrying.

Using Smudging or Incense as an Alternative Personal Cleanser

A quicker way of cleansing your personal aura or energy field and casting protection around yourself as a psychic shield is to use a sage or cedar herbal smudge stick or firm incense stick. You can do this straight after smudging the room, the table, and the tools.

Start by facing what is approximately North. Raise the smudge stick in front of you at about a 60-degree angle, and ask that Grandmother of the Snowy Places blesses and protects you. Turning clockwise, face East, raise the smudge, and ask that Brother Wind protects and blesses you. Turning clockwise to the South, raise the smudge as before and ask that Grandfather Sun protects and blesses you. Face West, raise the smudge, and ask that Sister Water protects and blesses you. Then facing North again, raise the stick vertically above your head and ask that Father Sky protects and blesses you; then point it downwards to ask for the protection and blessings of Mother Earth.

Finally, hold the smudge vertically in front of your body while facing North, and ask that your inner wisdom and wise self brings blessings and protection. Then, waft the smoking incense or smudge stick, still held in the hand you write with, in alternate counterclockwise and clockwise spirals around your body as if you were dancing, being careful not to bring the smoke too close to your face.

If you wish, you can create a cleansing chant to say or think as you smudge yourself, such as, "Bless and protect, guide and guard me from all harm." Return the lighted smudge or incense to the right side of the table as you face it; the fragrance helps to induce clairvoyance.

Invoking Blessings and Protection on Yourself

Instead of beginning by purifying yourself, you can start with a blessing. You can add this after the candle and incense lighting (see the next section). For special occasions you can add a blessings after the purification and incorporate it into the scrying opening or beforehand if you prefer.

The Celtic Circling Prayer

This is an informal blessing and is appropriate if you are working with a number of different people. It is also very protective for contacting your ancestors or Spirit Guides, or working with past lives.

Start by sitting or standing with your crystal point facing North and make clockwise circles with the crystal over the table and tools as you speak the blessing. This blessing can also be spoken outdoors. It was originally created for protecting an unfamiliar outdoor area by walking around the area in a circle three times clockwise while saying the words continuously.

When outdoors, you can walk around in an imaginary circle of light within which you will work, speaking the following words over and over again as a soft continuous chant while pointing the crystal directly ahead.

Circle this place
Mother, Father,
Keep harm without, keep peace within.
Circle this place
Father, Mother,
Bless and protect me here,
This day/this night.

The 4 Angels and the Archangel Invocation

The Archangel Invocation or Blessing is slightly more formal. It can be very helpful for those who are embarking upon reading for others for the first time or working with them in a healing environment. Again, it can be used outdoors.

The four traditional directional protective Archangels, Uriel, Raphael, Michael, and Gabriel, are pictured as sending rays of light upwards to form a shimmering star above the table or place you are working.

After or instead of the purification you can begin scrying by lighting the central candle and then in turn each of the angel candles from it. The angel candles would be set at the approximate direction around the outside of your table. For a special occasion use the four angel incenses, lighting each from its own angel candle, right after lighting the angel candle.

Uriel

Uriel, whose name means "Fire of God," is the Archangel of transformation and alchemy, and of the planet Mars.

Picture Uriel with an open hand holding a flame, dressed in rich, burnished gold and ruby red with a bright flame-like halo similar to a bonfire blazing in the darkness, and a fiery sword. He can be invoked separately for Earth scrying. His ray is dark red or indigo, and he brings the power of understanding and compassion to your clairvoyant powers.

Direction: North

Element: Earth

Candle color: Dark red

Incenses: Basil, copal, sandalwood, and ginger

Raphael

Raphael, whose name means "God has healed," is the Archangel of medicine, all forms of healing, travelers, and of the planet Mercury.

Picture him carrying a golden vial of medicine, with a staff to support travelers over stony ground, dressed in the colors of early morning sunlight, with a beautiful green or yellow healing ray emanating from his halo. He can be invoked especially for Air scrying and brings healing powers to your experience.

Direction: East

Element: Air

Candle color: Yellow or green

Incenses: Lavender, lily of the valley, pine, and thyme

Michael

Michael, whose name means "Who is like to God," is the supreme Archangel, Archangel of the Sun, and one of the chief dragon-slaying angels.

Michael is pictured with golden wings in red and gold armor with a sword, shield, and a green date branch, and carrying the scales of justice or a white banner with a red cross. He can be invoked for Fire scrying and emanates a gold or white ray. He brings clarity to your scrying experience.

Direction: South

Element: Fire

Candle color: Gold

Incenses: Chamomile, frankincense, orange, or rosemary

Gabriel

Gabriel is Archangel of the Moon. His name means "God Has Shown Himself Mightily." Archangel Gabriel carries God's messages.

Picture him clothed in silver or the blue of the night sky (also the color of his rays), with a mantle of stars and a crescent moon for his halo, a golden horn, a white lily (alternatively with a lantern in his right hand), and with a mirror made of jasper in his left. For this reason he can be invoked especially for mirror scrying, Water scrying, and moon scrying.

Direction: West

Element: Water

Candle color: Silver

Incenses: Eucalyptus, jasmine, lily, myrrh, lilac, and rose

The Archangel Invocation or Calling

- Stand in front of your table facing North. Light the Uriel candle and say, "Uriel, Archangel of Transformation, bless and protect me and my work this day/night."

- Then light the Raphael candle, moving clockwise in the approximate East. Say, "Raphael, Archangel of Healing, bless and protect me and my work this day/night."

- Light the Michael candle in the South. Say, "Michael, Archangel of the Sun, bless and protect me and my work this day/night."

- Finally light the Gabriel candle in the approximate West. Say, "Gabriel, Archangel of the Moon, bless and protect me and my work this day/night."

- Return to facing North and look upwards, saying, "And above me is the shining star."

As you say each line, picture each Archangel, guarding one of the Four Directions, and above you, a huge six-rayed star whose light shimmers in all directions.

If you are in a public place you can picture the Archangels and the rays of light and say the words in your mind without moving. Outdoors you would turn to face the Four Directions in turn. If you don't know the directions you can assign North ahead of you, East on the right hand as you face the chosen North, and so on. Use the same points for the Directions whenever you scry there.

Who Are My Guides?

I believe we are all guided and protected by spiritual beings from the moment our spirit enters our earthly body until we return to the spiritual world after death. Adults, as do children, have a Guardian Angel, as well as Spirit Guides. The angel may have revealed a name or may just be called "my blue angel," which often refers to the color ray with which the angel is surrounded.

Spend time during scrying or meditation identifying and getting to know your different spiritual companions and protectors. When you know them better you can ask for the help of a particular guide to assist with a scrying session, or leave it open and ask that you are guided "by whoever can best advise me at this time." (I have suggested books in the Useful Reading section if you wish to know more about angels and Spirit Guides.)

Spirit Guides

You can carry out scrying without reference to any Guides, Guardians, or angels. However, Spirit Guides do act as good protectors for any scrying work and will often lead your psychic eye and clairvoyant ear.

In terms of scrying, Spirit Guides are excellent for resolving practical matters or when you have a personal love problem. They are similar to a spiritual best friend, only with a wider overview. You may sense that one Spirit Guide communicates more strongly than others through scrying, and if you ask you may call him or her clairvoyantly using a dark mirror.

Spirit Guides don't have human bodies as such because they are pure spirit form, vibrating faster than the speed of light, and so they don't need a body. However, if you do see your guide in a crystal ball or mirror, he or she will often assume the form he or she took in his or her last life.

Deceased family members may act as guides to the living. You may be aware of the perfume scent of a deceased grandmother while scrying; then you know she is near and has a message for you.

Personal Ancestors

Alternatively, your permanent guide may be a genetic ancestor from centuries before who has chosen to help you because you are following a similar life path to his or hers on earth, or because you share elements of his or her personality.

Our personal guide may be a member of our soul family, a group of souls who travel though different lifetimes together occupying different roles according to the lessons to be learned. He or she has chosen to remain on the spiritual plane for a while or permanently to guide the members of the soul family currently on Earth.

Though we have one lifelong Guardian Angel and a Spirit Guide other guides and wise teachers do appear according to our needs and the stage of life we have reached.

Spiritual Ancestors

Your spiritual ancestor guide can be of great help in past-life scrying, whether it is personal issues in this lifetime that trouble you from years before, or spiritual development. He or she is not directly related to you by blood, but will be a wise man or woman from another culture or age who may appear to you regularly in dreams or scrying.

If you have not already encountered your spiritual ancestor, you may do so during scrying by asking in a dark mirror, a crystal sphere, water, a candle flame, or when using floating candles on water.

Usually this wise figure comes from a culture to which you have a special spiritual connection or affinity, often one associated with great wisdom, such as Ancient Egypt, the Viking world, China, or Native North America.

Angels

As you will see, I have referred to specific angels in different chapters (for example, Archangel Metatron the scribe, for scrying with inks).

However, for spiritual matters or to explore other dimensions, you can ask your Guardian Angel to assist and protect. Evidence through the ages gives remarkably consistent descriptions of the external appearance of angels. This would indicate that these higher beings do have an existence independent of human thought. However, angels have not lived on Earth (with the exception of Metatron and his twin Sandalphon).

Even the more approachable Guardian Angel is made of pure energy that vibrates at an even higher level than that of Spirit Guides or ancestors, and so they may be even harder to see; mostly they come across as light shimmers. The crystal ball or clear mirrors are good entry points for visions of your angel.

Opening Yourself to Your Clairvoyant Powers

This method uses the Far Eastern seven chakra energy system. The chakras are pictured as psychic whirling energy centers within our body that draw in energy from all around us, from Nature and other people, and from your angels and guides.

By opening your chakras before a reading, you are opening your spiritual energies to gain maximum impact from the scrying and higher sources of wisdom. (If you are interested in studying the aura and chakras, I have suggested books in the Useful Reading section at the end of this book.)

Begin by picturing red light pouring up from the Earth through your feet and legs and coiling around the small of your back, where it is said the Kundalini, or inner energy source we possess, rests waiting. If you are sitting down, you can locate

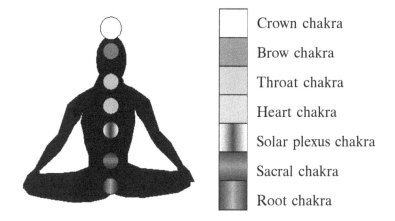

Crown chakra

Brow chakra

Throat chakra

Heart chakra

Solar plexus chakra

Sacral chakra

Root chakra

the Root or Base chakra around your perineum at the point your body touches the ground. This is the chakra that is connected to the physical body and your instincts. This is the seat of your physical senses and so it is the entry point of scrying.

Now imagine the red light spiraling upwards through different, small silvery energy channels at the front and back of your body, to meet in a rich orange and silver sphere just below your navel. This is your Sacral chakra and is the emotional and clairsentient center of your body where you automatically gain psychic impressions of people and places while scrying.

Now the red and orange light mix and pass through countless more spiraling channels until they reach your yellow solar plexus in the center of your stomach. This is where your psychokinetic powers (the power of the mind to move things) reside that guide your hand as it sprinkles herbs on water, shakes the candle wax, or swirls inks in precisely the right way to create the images you need to see the answer to your questions.

Each of these chakra centers, when activated, glow and whirl (described as whirling wheels of lotus petals).

The energy continues to spiral and rise via your body, hands, and arms to your green Heart chakra situated in the middle of your chest. The colors swirl and mingle as this chakra opens.

You have now reached the chakra where you begin to draw energy and light upwards and downwards from the cosmos via your higher chakras. The Heart is the seat of psychometric powers where you absorb information via your fingertips. It also connects you with evolved Nature beings and the wise ancestors, your own and those of other people, and your Guardian Angel and Spirit Guides. This energy continues to rise up through the chakras as energy channels to the Crown chakra; at the same time, energies begin to spiral down from the three upper centers into the Heart chakra, which is the power house and integrator of all the energies.

The Throat chakra immediately above the Heart chakra is blue and is centered in the middle of the throat. It controls clairaudience or psychic hearing to hear messages from your inner voice and higher beings. The Brow, or Third Eye chakra, is indigo or purple, and controls clairvoyance, psychic vision, and where all the other psychic abilities converge. This is in the center of the brow.

Finally, extending from the hairline up beyond the head is the highest Crown chakra, violet, merging with the gold and white of the cosmos. This is the pure Divine creative force and occasionally brings a flash of brilliant insight or awareness to your clairvoyant work and a sense of unity with all creation as you explore other dimensions.

Sit quietly and picture the psychic energies becoming pure white light and energy within you. If you touch your crystal ball, you may feel and see sparks between it and your fingertips.

Beginning Scrying

To begin the process, light your central candle when scrying indoors even during the day, unless the method calls for darkness, as with dark mirrors (Chapter 11).

I begin any psychic session whether alone, with a group, or just one other person, by lighting the central candle. If others are present I invite them to light a small candle from the central flame (and if a number of people are present, have them light from one another's candles). I ask each person to say, "I am (name) and I light this candle for (whatever they are most seeking from the scrying)." I do this when alone, using the main candle to center myself on the scrying process.

When You Get Stuck

You've cleansed, protected, called on your source of wisdom, amd lit what you should, and you start to look into the scrying surface—and look and look. Absolutely nothing comes. This happens to the most experienced clairvoyants, especially if you sense a client is not in the mood to be open. Use these steps to try and move the process along.

- Breathe in through your nose, counting in your mind *one and two and three and four*.
- Hold the breath, counting in your mind *one and two…*
- Breathe out through the nose, counting in your mind *one and two and three and four*.
- Finally, pause for the count of *one and two* before repeating the cycle.
- Repeat the cycle four or five times (subtly if you are not alone).
- Look into the scrying medium and picture a small pure white dot in the center that grows slowly into a sphere of light that covers a third of the inside or surface.
- Your first image should be in the white sphere.

After Scrying

Just as you would not leave the car engine running after driving or the front door open after your party guests had gone home, it is important, whether scrying indoors and out, to close down your spiritual energies so your mind is not buzzing all night or distracting you when it should be focusing on more mundane matters during the day. When you are done scrying, use the following steps.

- First, cleanse your tools as described in the individual chapters.

- Thank the Guardians who protected you during scrying and, if outdoors, bury a crystal or coin.

- Wish them goodbye, saying, "Until we meet again" to close the connection.

- Close down your own energy centers by passing your palm horizontally facing inwards over the center of your hairline. Picture the swirling white, violet, and gold sphere of life slowing down, and the soft blue velvet covering it.

- Next pass your hand over your Brow chakra and picture the purple and indigo swirling sphere of light slowing and being covered by deep blue.

- Then visualize the blue sphere in the center of your throat slowing and becoming covered by the velvet blue as your Throat chakra closes.

- Now allow the green whirling Heart chakra in the center of your chest to be slowed and covered in deep blue.

- Picture the deep blue light carrying the calmness down into the yellow Solar Plexus sphere in the center of your stomach, and slowing and closing this chakra.

- Next, the deep blue slows and covers the whirling orange and silver Sacral chakra just below your navel, and finally down to your feet, where at the small of your back, the red Root chakra is also slowed and covered. The Kundalini energy coils and sleeps once more until next you call it.

- ✍ Then, while sitting or standing, push down with your feet and keep your fingers pointing downwards with your hands at your sides, allowing any excess energy to flow back into the earth or floor.

- ✍ Alternatively, reverse the Archangel blessing, picturing the star above you fading and turning counterclockwise. Say, "Farewell until we meet again" to Gabriel, Michael, Raphael, and Uriel.

- ✍ End any scrying session with the blowing out of the candles and a private closing blessing, but leave the incense to burn through safely.

- ✍ Ring your bell or rattle around the space to close it for the day or night.

Scrying in a Hurry

When you only have five minutes to spare, use this highly protective and empowering ritual that can be substituted for personal cleansing and protection. It can be used outdoors if you take a small bottle of mineral water with you. I have also used it midway through a series of appointments to tune me back in after counselling a very troubled client.

Begin with the center of your hairline that represents the Crown chakra and your Evolved Self/Divine spark (picture a sphere of white, gold, and violet light). Touch it with a drop of water from your index finger of the hand you write with or your crystal point dipped into the water. Say, "Above me the Light." Then, in the same way, splash the center of your Brow for your Third or Clairvoyant Eye and picture the purple or indigo sphere. Say, "Within me the radiance." Touch your throat with the water (visualize a blue light) and say, "That I may speak wisely."

Finally, anoint the center of your chest if you are wearing something suitable or if you prefer, the insides of your wrists for your Heart chakra (visualize a green light). Say, "The love (or the truth) in my heart."

Chapter 3

Scrying With Water

Water scrying, or hydromancy, is the oldest and most popular source of clairvoyant visions in almost every culture. People have always revered water, which was essential for life, and natural water sources were thought to be the waters from the womb of the Earth Mother. Many other scrying arts, such as mirror and crystal spheres, ink, and oil readings, naturally follow from it.

Scrying with Water is as varied as the many kinds of water in nature: deep lakes; natural pools; sacred wells; bubbling streams; slow, silent rivers; rushing flowing watercourses, waterfalls; and the sea in all her moods and tides.

Water as a Source of Wisdom

Sacred wells have always been regarded as a place to seek knowledge from the future. Some looked to the Goddess, or in Christian times the saint to whom the well was often rededicated. In folk custom, people sought the fairy of the well. In pre-Christian times, priestesses at these wells were consulted by women on matters of fertility, health, love, and family matters.

A relic of this has survived in the folk custom—people often visit holy wells to gain knowledge of future partners. In North Kelsey, in Lincolnshire in Eastern England, girls would walk three times backwards around Maidens' Well and then look into the water to see the image of their true love, often unknown.

St. Catherine IV of Alexandria, the 4th-century patron saint of young women, also inspired maidenly prayers for love and marriage. On November 25th, her feast day, young spinsters would pray for a husband, at her wells and springs, similar to the one in the now ruined Abbey grounds at Cerne Abbas in Dorset in South West England, above which the chapel of St. Catherine formerly stood.

Young girls would turn around three times clockwise and ask St. Catherine for a husband, making the sign of the cross on their foreheads with the water. They would then look in the water to see an image of their future husband.

It was also said that visions could be seen by anyone gazing into Lady wells, an area that indicates the presence of a healing well, dedicated to the Virgin Mary, especially on Christmas morning when the star of Bethlehem could be seen in the water by those who were destined for a golden future. Also, if a pregnant woman or a woman trying to get pregnant saw the Star, she would give birth to a gifted child.

On May 1st, slow-moving rivers offer visions of the past, present, and future in quick succession if five white pebbles were dropped into the water as the first light came.

According to St. Augustine, who lived around 500 C.E., in Germany, ordinary women frequently studied the whirls and swirls of fast-flowing rivers, such as the Rhine, to gain wisdom from the water spirits. Needless to say, the saint did not approve.

Such practices of consulting water essences through scrying continue in folk custom even today, and modern scryers still drop coins in water as a way of paying tribute for the wisdom that will hopefully be found within the water.

The 4 Water Angels

Phul

Angel of the Lakes, Wells, and Still Waters. Visualize him standing directly to the North of the bowl (use approximate directions if you wish), with the bowl in the center of the table. Picture him as silvery blue, almost transparent. Use a single silver candle for him in the North.

Nahaliel

Angel of the Running Streams. Nahaliel is the younger brother of Trsiel, the Angel of the Rivers. Nahaliel stands in the East, to your right as you face North or approximate North. Nahaliel is quite misty with robes, wings, and a halo of soft green. Use a pale green or lilac candle to signify him.

Trsiel

Angel of the Rivers. Trsiel is angel of rivers large and small, and also estuaries where the river enters the sea. He stands directly behind you in the South as you are facing the North so you are within the angelic circle. Picture him in many shades of green with a halo of sparkling rainbow water drops. Use a dark green candle set directly in front of you on the table as you face North (though the angelic presence is behind you).

Rahab

Angel of the Sea. Rahab is the angel who retrieved the Archangel Raziel's book of wisdom from the deep. He stands in the West, to signify the ancient Element of Water. Picture him in deep blues and greens, striding over the white foamed waves with his billowing white wings similar to sails. Light a blue or turquoise candle on the West, in your left hand as you face North.

Attuning to Water Scrying

You can use water scrying for resolving absolutely any question. It is most effective for love, relationship, fertility, family, health and healing matters, for seeing other dimensions, and for uncovering secrets, or what has been lost. The more aware you are of images naturally occurring in water, the more easily you will adapt to more formal water scrying.

Water scrying is mainly a personal art for decision-making, rather than to advise others in a clairvoyant reading. However, it can be used by a group of people to make a joint decision. Using a large bowl, you stand around to scry for individual images you interpret together.

Whatever form of water scrying you attempt, you will need illumination on the water to provide the contrasting patterns of light and shadow that lead your physical eye to *see* the deeper psychic images.

Collecting water from a natural turbulent water source in a clear container is a popular method of water scrying because it allows the water to be studied at leisure in a more controlled setting. (See the section on sea scrying later in the chapter.)

You can wash the dishes or clothes by hand, and gaze into the suds and identify images. Alternatively, half-fill a washing up bowl or clear cooking dish and squirt a trail of dish detergent on to the surface of the water, allowing it to form swirling images. Do not worry about analyzing them.

Many people sit in a bath of warm water illuminated by candles, and move the bath foam around with their fingers to make shapes, patterns, and pictures.

While you are floating in a swimming pool, try scrying for pictures in the water. The results are best when the pool is illuminated by overhead lights or natural sunlight. Choose a time early or late in the day when the swimming pool is quiet and relatively empty of people. Otherwise, you can paddle out in a lake or the sea and sit in the shallow water gazing downwards through the clear water. If you don't like to swim, another option is to sail or row a boat on a lake and stay where it is still and deep and look downwards.

When abroad, visit sacred springs or special lakes or rivers, learn of their spirits and legends, and try scrying within them. Sometimes at sacred wells you can buy or collect the sacred water and you can add a little of this to your own indoor scrying water.

Spend time by different kinds of water, listening to the sounds of a river running over stones or the sea crashing on rocks, as these will hold messages about the images you see in the water.

When you find a water source that you like, visit it in different weathers and seasons, and see how images and sounds are affected by rain falling into a still pool, or the sound of the wind whipping up a waterfall. Even in the center of a city you can use pools and fountains in parks, garden ponds, small indoor water features, or an industrial river or canal with oil that forms rainbows on the surface.

Dedicating and Cleansing Your Scrying Bowl

Even if you work mainly with outdoor water sources, have a special water scrying bowl you keep with your scrying tools. It may be one you already possess in your ordinary crockery. Choose a clear glass, crystal, or pale or white ceramic bowl. It should be either cereal- or dessert-sized, or one similar to an old-fashioned fruit bowl. Once dedicated for scrying, you can keep it wrapped in a natural fabric when not in use. Blue would be a good color. The following ritual draws in the energies of the four main angels of the waters. You can also use this cleansing and dedication instead of empowering before any special water scrying.

The Ritual

- Put your scrying bowl in the center of the table half-filled with water, and set the four angel candles as I have suggested. To the right of the bowl set a small dish of salt.

- Cleanse the scrying bowl by dropping a pinch of salt into the water and swirling it around three times counterclockwise, three times clockwise, and three times counterclockwise, saying, "May visions within this bowl be pure and true."

- Light the silver candle and say, "May Phul, angel of still waters, bless this bowl and my scrying."

- Light the pale green or lilac candle from the silver one and say, "May Nahaliel, angel of the running waters, bless this bowl and my scrying."

- Light the dark green candle from the light green one and say, "May Trsiel, angel of the flowing waters, bless this bowl and my scrying."

- Finally, light the blue or turquoise candle from the dark green one and say, "May Rahab, angel of the oceans, bless this bowl and my scrying." You can substitute blue candles for each angel if you wish.

- Pour out the salt water, rinse the scrying bowl with clear water, and then add your scrying water.

- Empower the bowl by saying the four angel names in order, silently if you prefer, "Phul, Nahaliel, Trsiel, and Rahab, bring blessings." Do this after the rinsing and adding the scrying water.

- For general scrying, cleanse the bowl as previously mentioned and then move to this empowering stage without using the candles or the longer angel chants.

After scrying, to remove the psychic impressions, add a pinch of salt to the water, swirl it three times counterclockwise, then rinse it, pour it out, and leave the bowl to dry naturally.

Seeing Images in Water

The principle of clear water scrying is similar to the physiological /psychological ganzfeld effect where you stare at a blank wall or ceiling, and, after a time, images appear on the blank surface. The psychic eye uses the same principle to cast up clairvoyant images in clear water. These are not random, but directed by and from your unconscious wisdom or higher sources of wisdom to give you the information you need.

Do not expect to see clear scenes as though peering through a window. Images for clear water scrying are more akin to those seen through a car windshield on a rainy day without the wipers on.

When you are confident you can ask a question as you look into the water. Close your eyes between images and, if you wish, pass the hand you write with counterclockwise three times closely over the bowl of water to clear the previous impressions. This is not necessary outdoors.

Afterward, cleanse the bowl as suggested before and, where possible, throw away scrying water outside the house on the ground or, if indoors, under a flowing tap.

Indoor Scrying

During the day, work with sunlight on clear water in your glass or white scrying bowl. Some scryers believe it is better to work just before sunrise or just after sunset when the world is quieter and the conscious mind more relaxed.

If it is nighttime and the moon is shining, use moonlight reflected in the water source or substitute with two or three flickering candles, unless you suffer from a medical condition that makes flickering lights a problem for you. You can create the flickering effect by opening a window slightly to let the moonlight and breeze in.

Place the candles so that the light is seen moving on the water. The candles should be the only light. If the dawn light breaks during early morning scrying, you can extinguish the candles.

Darkened but not black water can be used. It is traditionally darkened by adding an infusion of mugwort, thyme, or sage, all natural divinatory herbs. To make the infusion, add one to two small spoons of dried herbs to a normal-sized cup or three to a mug, pour on boiling water, stir it, and cover for about five minutes for a relatively light infusion. You can use the kind of dried herbs you buy in the spices section of a supermarket. Increase the proportions as necessary. Strain off the herbs and leave the liquid to cool.

Add the infusion to the bowl so it is about a third full, and then add clear water until the bowl is about half full. Swirl the water so the two mix. The water should be colored, but not too dense. Illuminate it with candles or sunlight. For an easy alternative, you can use herbal tea bags. Experiment with making herbal teas so you get different shades of water. Try chamomile, rosehip, peppermint, and lemon for different fragrances. Discard the tea bag.

Quickly stir the bowl of water in daylight or, better still, in light directly from the sun, several times clockwise with a clear quartz crystal point or the index finger of the hand you write with.

You can drop up to six small clear quartz crystals or citrine into the bottom of the bowl after adding the water for additional sparkles, and also to read the ripples (see the following pages). A group could each drop a crystal in the larger bowl to perceive an image.

You can also scry with red wine, traditionally in a metal goblet, or use a smoked brandy glass, half filled and lit by a horseshoe of candles. Wine is read by swirling it around in the glass as you hold it in the hand you write with.

Burning incense or fragrance oil is a good background for indoor scrying, as it helps to raise your consciousness from the everyday thoughts to the spiritual planes. While scrying, experiment with different fragrances until you find one that heightens your awareness, but is not too overpowering. Floral fragrances work well for water scrying of all kinds. If you use incense you can see images in the smoke as well as in the water.

Outdoor Water Scrying With Moving Water

When outdoors, ask permission of the local Water spirits and make a traditional offering of a coin, a small item such as a silver or gold earring, or some flowers or seeds, before beginning. If it is not polluted, you can collect water in a bowl rather than scrying with the water source if you prefer. You can also seek the blessing of the appropriate Water angel.

Use slowly moving water when there is a light breeze. However, a faster-moving stream or river with a bed of stones will add the clairaudient aspect. Before scrying, stand with your eyes closed to tune into the sound of water bubbling over stones. Afterward, when you have seen enough images, close your eyes once more and let the water speak to you.

In any case of water scrying, imagine you are floating with the water in your mind. You may find it easier to sway slightly or move your hands rhythmically as you gaze into the water.

Focus on the area in the center of the ripples and let the image form from light and shadows. A fountain will cast up pictures in the foam, especially if you watch the bubbles of water where they merge together and the sun is shining on them. Fountains that change color at night are also excellent for scrying.

While the water is still moving, look into it and read rapidly, one after the other, images formed by light and shadows. This method stops your conscious mind from intruding. The images will be quite fleeting, so once you are seeing images, you may prefer to work with still water.

Try the three stones method from ancient Greece. Quickly cast three stones one after the other into still water. Although the original format advocated one square and one triangular stone, as well as one round stone, three round ones are best, all the same size. As the ripples form, allow a picture to emerge on the surface of the water and then fade as the ripples fade. Cast three more to add to the information if you wish and keep throwing in threes until you have your answers. If you are going to use a lot stones, stony beaches by small lakes are ideal; or take a bag of pebbles if the shore is sandy or grassy.

Waterfalls will cast up images and give clairaudient messages in the roaring water. Try scrying first from a bridge overlooking the waterfall, and then from partway up, and finally from the base. Take an image reading from each position and put the wisdom together with the messages.

If you can safely do so, get behind the waterfall, as the ancient Celtic Druids and Druidesses used to do and look out through the wall of water. Contrast a smaller waterfall with a huge one such as Niagara Falls.

Do not worry if at first you only see sparks of light and mists that clear to form shapes and patterns. You may get impressions of what you think you saw, but may be unaware of actually seeing an image. This is because your clairvoyant eye is transmitting, but too fast for your conscious mind to process the imagery. In time your processing abilities will become more accustomed to dealing with psychic material via water.

Outdoor Scrying With Still Water

When you feel confident, gaze into unmoving water in a lake or deep pool and breathe gently, slowly, and regularly, picturing your own boundaries melting and flowing into the water so that you become a part of the water itself. Bright sunlight or moonlight is perfect. Clouds reflected in water will also create images.

If you are not seeing images, exhale very slowly from your mouth towards the water similar to a sigh. After each in breath, push the clairvoyant image filtered via your psyche onto, and within, the surface of the water. Name the image you have breathed into the water, in your mind or as part of the sigh as you are exhaling. Take another slow in breath, exhale, name, and continue. When you have the rhythm and images coming fast, breathe slowly and normally and the images will come much slower on the surface of, or within the water, often as faint, shimmering light reflections and shadowy flickering forms. You can also try this technique with a bowl of water indoors or out.

Sea Scrying

Sea scrying can be practiced either in a rock pool, in sea water in a bowl, or by looking at the ocean. The ideal conditions for this activity would be sunlight, moonlight, or a windy day when clouds are reflected in the waters, and the wind is blowing the waves around. If the sea is very calm you can paddle out and look down into the water as you sit or stand in the shallows.

A method employed by ancient sea witches, which I practice because I live very close to the shore, involves the use of a large, old-fashioned fish or punch bowl. Mine is made of yellow smoked glass. In earlier times, these were called witch bowls.

Sea witches would also use old-fashioned dark glass fishing floats by holding them so they were half submerged in the water and looking within them.

Deep, round, glass bowls can be found in many parts of the world, often sold at garage sales or antique markets for cheap.

Dedicate, cleanse, and empower the bowl at the beginning of each session by immersing it in the sea three times and asking the blessings of Rahab and the local sea guardian. Collect shells or very small white stones from the shore before beginning and put them in the bottom of your bowl. Wade out into the water to partly fill the bowl with sea water and then sit on the shore close to the water, swishing the shells in the light to combine psychic sound and vision.

I would highly recommend sitting on the shore as sunlight or moonlight fills the water. Sometimes you pick up bits of sea plants or even tiny fish with the water. Afterward, tip the shells and stones back into the water.

An offering is cast after scrying the seventh or ninth wave. You take the wave as it almost reaches shore as wave number one, then looking out to sea start counting the waves coming in. The seventh and ninth are associated with sea spirits and are good for receiving offerings. A tiny pearl or small aquamarine stone, some white flowers, or small piece of fruit are especially appropriate offerings.

Then immerse the bowl a final time in the water. You can rinse it with clear water later. For a very special occasion, after the scrying, find a large piece of driftwood to make an offerings boat. On it place the offering you brought along, plus something that was cast up on the shore, something that belongs to the sea, a beautiful shell, a small piece of seaweed, a naturally occurring quartz crystal, or a feather from a seagull.

If you are working in the early morning or after twilight, light a small, flat beeswax candle or tea light on the wood. Paddle out or wait for the seventh or ninth wave to hit the shore and carefully launch your offerings boat.

Scrying With the Ocean or an Inland Sea

The sea has her moods as well as her changing tides, so scrying directly with the waves is the most powerful of all water scrying. Where possible, try scrying in all her different moods and tides, and always respect the powers and dangers of the ocean. Though you can ask any question of the sea at any time, if you work with her specific moods and tides your results will be even more accurate. Call out the question or ask that you are shown what most you need to know.

First close your eyes to attune to the sound. Open your eyes and focus on the seventh or ninth wave. As it rolls in, use this to see an image either within the foam or shimmering within the wave as it rises and falls. As an alternative, you can scan an area of the sea directly ahead and use the white tipped waves to form moving images.

If the sea is calm, focus on an area of brightness in the center of the horizon as you stand on the shore and allow the light, cloud formations, and shadows reflected on the water to form an image on the surface.

A Calm Sea

Ingoing or outgoing, a calm sea is ideal for questions about harmony and peace-making, bringing stability into your life, finances, or career; questions about love and happiness; family matters; children and pets; travel; and holiday plans.

A Stormy Sea

Ingoing or outgoing, this is the sea to ask about any kind of major changes, including relocation, justice, independence, matters of self esteem, bullying in any setting, overcoming obstacles, fame, success, or recognition.

A Moonlit Sea

A relatively calm sea is good for questions of love, romance, marriage and fidelity, fertility, mothers and motherhood, children of any age, healing, and mending quarrels.

A Sunlit Sea

This kind of sea for good for questions about success, ambition, creativity, the performing arts, learning and examinations, happiness, health, energy levels, property and finances, sports and competitions, and finding what is lost.

The Sea on a Cloudy Day

This kind of sea will help with matters of uncertainty or that are slow to come to fruition, obstacles, all changes, recovery from loss, illness, or debt, endings of all kinds, and secrets both to be revealed and which should be kept, including secret love.

Incoming Tide

This situation is good for new ventures, career, business, self-employment, creative projects and new beginnings, matters where luck or speculation are involved and so need to be predicted, health, justice, official matters, and all financial affairs. The more urgent or immediate the question, the higher the tide you should scry with.

The Slack Tide

The short period called "slack tide" can last an hour or more, and is one of magical balance. It occurs between high and low tides as they prepare to turn. During the slack tide there is no real current flow, which makes it good for all questions about weighing two options, choices of all kinds; priorities or divided loyalties; disputes with neighbors, colleagues, or friends; dual careers; or commitments or love triangles.

The Outgoing/Ebb Tide

Use the ebb tide for concerns about debt, injustice, addictions, pain, guilt, blame, abusive or destructive relationships, loneliness, ill health, financial or career problems, security, and protection. The lower the tide, the less urgent or more distant the matters under question should be.

Choosing Special Waters for Scrying

You can use absolutely any clear clean water for scrying and, as I said earlier in the chapter, if you are using a container, taking the water from a natural water source makes the scrying very powerful.

Rain water collected before it touched the ground—that is, in water tubs or in bowls—is a traditional source of scrying water. With the increase in acid rain, you can add a single drop of your favorite flower or tree essence to the water before scrying to spiritually purify it.

Tap water can be used for cleansing and scrying as long as it is from a bubbling tap. However, some practitioners prefer filtered or bottled water; a number of bottled waters on the market actually come from healing or sacred springs.

Spiritually cleanse water for scrying or for anointing your chakras by passing a pendulum over it counterclockwise three times, hold the pendulum up to the light, and then pass it three times clockwise over the scrying water to energize it.

Scrying water can be filled with many natural powers, such as crystalline, sun, moon, rain, melted snow, storm, and winds to make it suitable for specific purposes.

You can anoint yourself with any of the waters after scrying to fill yourself with its powers and to bring your decisions into practice in the days ahead.

Sun Water

Sun water is good for all the purposes listed under the sunlight scrying section and can be used on dark, dull days. It is especially good if you feel anxious or tired, and will help you to see the positive aspects and openings ahead during scrying.

Make sun water by putting out a clear glass bowl or jug of water in the open air covered by mesh to stop any particles or insects from falling in. Leave it from dawn until noon or when the sun is directly overhead in your time zone (in a place that catches the morning sunlight). In winter, when dawn is later and solar energies are weaker, allow it to catch as much daylight as you can. In climates where there is not much light, leave it for two days.

Before beginning, stir the water three times clockwise with a clear crystal pendulum or pointed clear quartz crystal, and ask that the sun fill the water with power and healing. Name any special scrying purpose for which you are making the water. Stir the water again three times clockwise with your clear crystal pendulum or pointed quartz crystal. It is best if the sun is shining in the water during this time. Again, name the focus and the purpose of the water if there is one.

Using a clear glass jug and a filter, bottle the water in small clear, yellow or gold-colored glass bottles with stoppers or screw-top lids. Sun water will keep its power for three weeks in a fridge or a cool place.

Moon Water

Moon water can be used for all the purposes listed for moonlight scrying, and also whenever you are feeling sad, lonely, or out of harmony with your body or with other people. Moon water is also good for perceiving visions of other dimensions. Moon water is at its most potent when made on the night of the full moon or during a partial or total lunar eclipse. You can also make it two or three days before the full moon if the skies are clear and the moon shining brightly.

On the night of the full moon (it raises around sunset), set a silver-colored or clear crystal bowl outdoors where the moonlight can shine on it. Fill it halfway with still mineral water. If possible, use water from a sacred source or a few drops of water from a holy well. You can substitute with bubbling tap water also.

Stir the water nine times counterclockwise with a silver-colored (the color and metal of the moon) paper knife or an amethyst crystal point. Ask the Moon Mother to bless the water and those who use it. Leave the bowl in position, covered with fine mesh, overnight. In the morning, using a glass jug and filer, pour the water into small blue, silver, dark, or frosted glass bottles that you can seal and keep in your fridge or a cool place until the next full moon night. Pour any water that is left at the end of the moon period into the ground before the moon rises on the full moon night.

Storm and Wind Water

Use wind and storm water for questions about issues where you need courage, concerning a major change in your life, for matters of identity, independence, bullying, or abuse in any form; also use them for questions about how to overcome obstacles or opposition and new beginnings.

You will need a large, wide-necked glass jar with a lid (cook-ware jars are ideal) so that the jar will not become overfilled if it rains. In advance, dig a hole in the earth deep enough to hold the jar securely, or find a sheltered corner outdoors where it will not blow over. Half-fill the jar with water and, when a storm or high winds begin, swirl the sealed jar three times clockwise, followed by three times counterclockwise. When the storm or high winds die down, hold the jar and reverse the order of shaking.

Use a filter to bottle the water in dark-colored bottles. That water will last about a week in a cool place, and any left should be cast to the winds with thanks, saying, "Return to your element."

Rain Water

Rain water is good for all questions concerning the environment, about corruption or deceit, about estrangements or misunderstandings, for health issues, for slow-moving or stagnant matters, for the return of what is lost, and for connecting psychically with people far away. This is the easiest of waters to make because all you need to do is collect it.

You can leave it in the container until you need it or fill small, clear glass bottles with it. If you can, add some morning dew collected from leaves or flowers with an eye dropper.

Snow Water

Snow water is obviously seasonal, though in parts of North America, Northern and Eastern Europe, the Baltic, and parts of Scandinavia there may be several months of snow each year. If you live in an area where there is no snow you can allow the snowy kind of ice from around your freezer shelves to melt naturally, or use ice cubes.

You can use snow water for any kind of scrying with water, but especially to find answers about quarrels, rejections past or present, emotional coldness between people, favoritism, frozen feelings, and lack of commitment.

Whether you use actual snow or ice from a freezer, you will need a metal bowl (stainless steel is ideal) if you are going to allow the snow to melt naturally. Use it immediately as ice water rapidly loses its power. Any old saucepan will do for melting snow over a flame if you are in a hurry. Stir it regularly in both directions, however many times you are comfortable with, and leave it to cool before using. Snow water cannot be kept.

Crystalline Waters

Waters in which crystals have been soaked are one of the oldest and most potent sources of scrying water, and are good both for anointing yourself and pouring into a bath. You can even drink them to endow you with the positive qualities of the crystal to further the decisions made during scrying.

You only need small crystals and a variety of glass containers and stopper or screw-top bottles in which to make your crystal waters. However, if you are going to make the waters directly in the bottles, you need ones with necks wide enough.

For crystal waters use filtered or still mineral water and rounded crystals. Be sure to wash them well before using for scrying. You will need one crystal the size of a nickel per tall mug of water (increase proportionally as required). Leave it for eight hours. Sparkling crystals such as clear quartz or citrine love sunlight for at least part of the time, and amethyst or rose quartz love moonlight, if possible.

Remove the crystal(s) or filter the water into smaller bottles. Crystal waters will last about three or four weeks.

Seeing Other Dimensions in Water

Stories of underwater kingdoms and lands reached by climbing down a sacred well are ways of explaining how we can access spiritual realms. By gazing deep into water, and also delving deep within our own subconscious mind, we can access the wisdom of all times and all places past, present, and future.

Many legends and fairytales tell of lands and Shamans, the magical priests/healers that are still found in indigenous societies from Siberia to sub-Saharan Africa. Shamans frequently dive down while in a trance into water holes or the sea to ask the ancient water mothers to release the fish and mammals, and to ask about the well-being of the people.

You can see other dimensions, angels, ancestors, and Spirit Guides by gazing deep into clear, still water lit by the moon or a bowl of clear water by candlelight. Ask for whom you wish to see, or to see a past world of which you were a part of. Press your hands over your eyes for a minute or two while visualizing the spiritual being or allowing an image of the past world to develop. Take your hands away, clap them over the water, and look deep. You will be rewarded by a vision that may fade and reform for several minutes. You will almost certainly hear words in your mind to expand the vision.

Chapter 4

Scrying With Fire

Pyromancy is the traditional name for the art of divination by fire. We know that fire was discovered by humans before 800,000 B.C.E. and evidence of actual hearths have been found as far back as 400,000 B.C.E. in ancient China. Therefore, we can only guess the antiquity of the earliest sacred fire ceremonies. But it is conceivable that people from early times would have sat in the darkness and looked at the pictures made by flames. They may have huddled, half asleep around the hearth fire or outdoors during a long watch, by a fire intended to keep away fierce predators. The images they saw in the flames and embers may have answered questions about their lives, looking similar to dreams. When there were no other lights, except perhaps a fire tallow lamp, the fire images must have seemed even more brilliant.

Fire and Prophecy

In a number of cultures women acted as guardians of fires. They tended the hearth fire, which was the heart of the home, to welcome home living family members and, it was once believed, the deceased wise ancestors and family guardians. In ancient Greece, a bride would take fire from her mother's hearth to keep Hestia the fire goddess's flame alight in her marital home and transfer protection and good fortune to the new hearth.

In Rome, Vesta, the goddess of fire, was similar to Hestia, deity of the family hearth and of sacred fires. The Eternal Flame of Rome was kept burning in the round temple at the foot of the Palatine Hill tended by Vesta's specially dedicated virgins.

The Eternal Flame was kept burning, until 380 C.E. Its priestesses were also fire prophetesses, making offerings to the protective deities of the state, as well as to Vesta, Mars, Jupiter the Father God, and Minerva, who was the goddess of justice and wisdom.

Changes in the pattern of flames and intensity of sacred and festival fires, especially in response to offerings cast on them, indicated the actions of the deities upon the coming harvest and planned military strikes.

Because of its volatile and unpredictable nature, fire was seen as a perfect medium for interpreting omens. In earlier times, sacrificial fires were considered the most potent to study, including way the flames burned and the direction of the smoke. The future, or at least the specific event under question, was considered promising and the deities favorable if a fire burned vigorously and any offerings were quickly consumed.

Festival Fires and Scrying

Nyd, or ceremonial fires, were kindled in Celtic times with nine different kinds of wood, using sticks that were rubbed together or a more elaborate oaken spindle as an alternative.

The fires were renamed to fit in with Christian festivals, for example the Easter Eve fires and the Midsummer St. John's Eve fires that replaced the Spring Equinox fires and the pre-Christian Summer Solstice.

Charred sticks were taken from the festival fire and placed on newly kindled home fires or kept through the year as protection against thunderstorms. Christian clergy continued the earlier practices of predicting the success of the harvests or herds in the season ahead in the seasonal fires. The tradition has continued in folk custom until the present day especially in lands where people of Celtic origin live.

The Judas Fires were the Christianized version of the Spring Equinox fires, when a scarecrow saved from the previous harvest was burned around March 21st to represent the return of the corn spirit to the ground, after the earlier sacrifice of the corn spirit (the end of August) as the last sheaf of grain was cut. The ashes were scattered on the fields to bring fertility in the spring. The straw figure was later renamed after Judas, the disciple who betrayed Jesus. The ceremony was very popular in German and Western Europe right through to the 1900s, where a straw man was burned on Easter Eve in Germany and the Netherlands was considered especially prophetic. The straw man may recall a long-distant pre-Christian human sacrifice of a local criminal or a willing more noble victim in savage times to bring fertility to the fields.

The Christianized Easter Eve fire lit outside a church would be used to relight all the candles in the church as Easter morning dawned, a custom now being revived in parts of America and Europe.

Folk Wisdom and Fire Scrying

Ordinary people, as well as seers, divined the fate/destiny of future plans by observing the flames of burning torches or by throwing powdered black pitch or tar onto outdoor fires. Sometimes the charred stick brought home from the Easter or Midsummer fires would be held in the hearth fire until it kindled, and a vision of the future 12 months in advance was seen by the family. If the tar on an outdoor fire caught fire and flamed quickly, the outcome of any planned individual, family, or community action was considered favorable.

Another form of fire divination involved interpreting pictures in the glowing embers of a fire. This was practiced in the home around the hearth or within the flames of a wood-burning stove to answer family questions. This form of fire scrying continues today, not only with the flames of a wood-burning stove in Scandinavian homes or the open hearth fire, but 21st-century style using glowing barbecue coals in a deep dome barbecue.

Fire was also used by young people in Eastern and Western Europe, right through to the 1900s, to discover about love and fidelity. For example, Halloween used to be called Nut-Crack Night in the UK. It is told that to discover whom you will marry, you should name each hazelnut you put in the fire after one of your suitors or people you like. The nut that cracks first will give the name of your true and lasting love.

At other times of the year, a single nut can be used to see if a named person is interested in you and if the relationship will develop. A nut that does not crack but just smolders and burns away generally indicates what you may know in your heart: Someone you desire is attached and probably will not leave his or her present partner to be with you

In another form of the Halloween game, five unmarried people play. Five nuts are thrown on the fire, one by each person. The first nut to crack belongs to the first person to marry, the second nut to crack foretells a long and lucky journey for its owner, the third will get money, the fourth will find love from overseas, and the fifth will discover many secrets that will open the doors of opportunity. You can add nuts for as many people as you wish and add different qualities or pieces of luck.

A third version of this ritual involves a man and woman. They both place a nut side by side in the fire and declare their love for each other. If the nuts glow and burn steadily, their relationship will be a calm, harmonious one. If the nuts fly apart or crack suddenly, the relationship will be a tempestuous but passionate one. If the nuts fuse together, then love will be lasting. If the nuts fuse but then split off in different directions, the number of new fire trails will indicate the number of children in the future. If the nuts just smolder, the relationship may need more input and time together, especially if one of the nuts does not ignite.

Fire Divination in India and Tibet

In India, the great fire god was Agni. He ruled not only over the fires of lightning and heaven, but the hearth and sacred fires on Earth, carrying offerings and prayers from humans to the gods on the dark canopy of smoke from mortal fires. Offerings to the fire deity were the first act of morning devotion as the sun rose in homes and temples (see also Chapter 1).

Tibetan fire scrying begins with the invocation of the fire spirits. The omens differ slightly from those of the Western tradition, so see which system seems right for you or take the best out of both. The importance is consistency, and once you have established a system of meanings that works well for you (record these in your scrying journal), they will become accurate. You can apply them to a whole fire or the area where you cast your stick/offerings.

- A bright, long-lasting, golden, orange-colored flame without smoke or crackling that either burned to the right or upwards in a single point, offers a positive affirmation to the question that prompted the divination.

- A white, gentle flame indicates that any past omissions or unkind deeds by yourself or others should now be left behind as they are holding the future back.

- A yellow flame promises power and wealth; a red flame success; and clear, smokeless blue, good health and fertility.

⌒ If the fire blazes fiercely with dark, smoky flames and there is no obvious pollutant of the material used, it warns to avoid self-delusion or to beware of the less-than-open attitude of others.

Beginning Fire Scrying

You can practice fire scrying on a bonfire in the garden, on a fire lit on the shore of a lake or by the ocean, on a domestic hearth fire or a wood-burning stove, or in a fire created in a small incinerator or metal garden burner. Alternatively, light a huge candle in a large metal pot filled with sand. Candles are best in a sheltered place outdoors or, if indoors, with a light breeze so the candle flickers. If it is nighttime, shadows will cast images as the flame moves.

A small, specially designed fire dish is wonderful for all outdoor and garden work so you can safely and easily light a fire anytime. I have seen beautiful dish-shaped copper fire dishes on metal legs for sale in garden centers, which are not expensive and need no adaptation. However, you can substitute any large fireproof metal dish with either a large cast iron wok or the bottom half of a domed, iron barbecue, again the kind with legs.

A Mexican/Spanish-style garden chiminea is also a good source of divinatory fire and these are widely obtainable, as are the less exotic, cheaper incinerator bases for burning garden waste.

If you use a traditional wood-burning stove for indoor work, the glass cover will cast added reflections, which are good especially for seeing images in the flames.

Choosing the Right Occasion

Fires can be lit on the evenings before special occasions or, if you prefer, the evening of a festival. I have listed energies that are strongest at these festivals but you can use any festival fire to ask about any purpose:

- **New Year's Eve:** Good for discovering the year ahead.

- **Candlemas Eve (December 31st or February 1st):** For new trust, new love, or rekindling an existing relationship. For making plans, and artistic and literary ventures.

- **Easter Eve or Spring Equinox (around March 21st):** For putting new beginnings into motion, developing love, and attracting health and money.

- **May Eve (April 30th, the pre-Christian Beltane, the beginning of the Celtic summer):** For fertility in every way, creativity, and passion.

- **The Summer Solstice Eve (around June 20th), St. John's, or Midsummer Eve (June 23rd):** For power, career success, fidelity, and marriage.

- **Lughnasadh (the first harvest; July 31st):** For justice, business partnerships, travel, house moves, and property matters.

- **Autumn Equinox, the second harvest (around September 22nd; that marks the beginning of the longer nights and colder days):** For reconciliation, for reaping rewards and letting go of what is destructive or no longer useful, and for healing.

- **Halloween or Samhain (October 31st):** For contact with the ancestors and Guides, as well as discovering secrets and recovering what is lost.

- **Christmas Eve or Midwinter Solstice (around December 21st when early peoples believed the sun was dying on the shortest and darkest day of the year):** For finding the way forward with matters that seem hopeless, for wishes and gifts sought, and giving to others, chronic health concerns, discovering about absent friends or family members, and for wisdom from angels.

⮠   Personal anniversaries, birthdays, the night before
    a wedding, to celebrate a birth or a family mem-
    ber leaving home, and even a divorce are all good
    times for fires and fire scrying. You can add many
    occasions of your own. Invite as many people as
    you wish, or you can work alone at any time you
    need answers or seek illumination.

Asking Questions

When working outdoors, whatever the occasion or fire source,
always ask for permission from the Land Guardians to use the place
and, if creating a fire, be very careful about leaving the land as you
found it after you are done. In a group, appoint one or two earthly
Fire Guardians to prepare the site and fire. Add fuel regularly and
be sure that the fire does not get out of hand. Afterward, clear the
site and make sure the fire is out.

Once the fire is burning, begin by throwing a handful of salt
on the fire, asking that your visions (and visions of those present)
may only consist of what is good. Then you and each person
present should in turn throw a handful of fragrant herbs on the
fire, choosing those with natural kinship to fire, such as basil,
fennel, or mint, or the divinatory ones, such as parley, sage,
rosemary, and thyme.

Though it is not safe to throw tar, pitch, or any other flam-
mable substance to make a fire flare, you can cast pine cones or
nuts onto the fire and see if they crack open or instantly flare;
that will indicate the swift resolution of a matter under question.

When the offerings are consumed, ask your question as you
poke the fire with a long fallen stick, if possible found near the
site, and add more herbs or wood to the fire.

Then cast the stick into the fire and look into the place it
burns, studying first the movement of the fire in that area or,
when you have a small fire, the pattern of the whole fire. You
can use the traditional interpretations following this section and,

as the fire dies down a little, in the place where the stick was added, look into the embers of the fire for images that will further your insights. When you have your answers, thank the Fire Guardians and offer some final dried herbs on to the fire as it grows low. You can ask further questions by adding more offerings and sticks.

When everyone has asked their questions, leave the fire to burn or burn out according to its purpose. Indoor fire should always be left to burn away naturally. If you are outdoors near a natural water source, such as a lake, cast any leftover herbs onto the waters and take some lake or sea water to put out the fire. The hiss of smoke will give final insights. As an alternative, you can also cover it with earth.

When the fire is cool, scoop up a few of the ashes into a small bag, especially if you lit your fire on the night of a festival. Make sure the ashes are cool before you do this. Bury a few of the ashes in the garden or a large growing pot to symbolically transfer the fertility of the venture you asked about. This will also dispel negative energies of the occasion into the natural growth cycle of the plant or to Mother Earth as she sees fit.

Clearing the site and thanking the guardians is essential to ensuring that the energies remain totally positive and the earthly Fire Guardians can organize everyone present. You can modify this for an indoor fire, but should always begin and end by asking permission of the House Guardians and the spirits of the fire and make offerings of herbs or dried flower petals. End by thanking the guardians and leaving the fire to burn away naturally.

Interpreting Fire

The traditional Westernized system is made up of the old mean-ings from ancient Persia, Greece, and Rome, and the folk tradi-tions of Eastern and Western Europe and Scandinavia. It has evolved over the years and will provide a basis for your own obser-vations. Fires should be studied in relatively calm conditions, as a high wind will cause the flames to bend or flare dramatically.

You can apply these meanings to the whole fire, especially if the fire is small, or if you are working alone or in a larger group.

- If a fire is difficult to light (or the offerings are slow to burn), unless the wood is damp, it suggests you may have to try several times or put a lot of effort into a venture.

- It is a good omen if the fire burns clear, meaning the flames are transparent rather than dark red or yellow, and the fire crackles.

- The swiftness of results can be calculated by the speed the fuel/stick/offerings are consumed and the intensity of the flames.

- A fire that burns silently and seems unduly blown about, or is slow to consume any offerings/sticks cast on it, indicates that the coming days and events need persistence and caution.

- If flames are mainly central (whole fire), pay attention to resolving the present issues before moving on.

- If flames are to the right (whole fire), then the past may still be excessively influencing the present.

- If flames areto the left (whole fires), focus on the future and make the first steps towards the desired changes.

- If a fire (whole fire) seems to burn low very quickly, then the venture or relationship under question may not last.

- A constantly spitting fire/area around your offerings/stick (unless you have used a wood you know spits a lot), indicates that there may be some initial opposition, spite, gossip, or unvoiced resentment that you feel needs to be expressed.

- Very sparking, sparkly flames promise recognition and rewards for efforts, and maybe even fame or instant success with a creative or performing venture.

- If the sparks fly in all directions, travel, house moves, or life changes are indicated.

- A fire/area of fire that suddenly flares upwards without any obvious reason, such as sudden gusts of wind, heralds unexpected success or passion.

- When working with a concentrated source of flame, such as a candle, the area of the stick, or a small fire, flames that rise to a point promise power and renewal; a clearly divided flame source; divisions, delays, and quarrels; and three divisions mean increased resources and growing success.

- Stressful times or financial difficulties are foretold by the bending of the main flame in the area of the stick/offerings if there is not a strong wind source. This indicates the need for forethought or a change of direction to ensure you are not going to try to do too much too quickly.

Finding Images in Fire

In childhood we often saw fire fairies and their realms in an open fire or within the burning wood stove in winter. Fire Elementals, such as the legendary salamander fire lizard people, can also be seen clairvoyantly in sources of fire and occasionally around candles. You can gain extra information by looking for actual images deep within the fire, especially around the base of the flames of an outdoor fire or a wood-burning stove or hearth fire. This is true clairvoyant fire scrying.

Fire dishes, chiminea, and barbecues with glistening fat on the glowing coals are also good for perceiving symbols, as is a gently flickering candle flame, where you look in the area round the flame or deep into the center of the flame. Most of all, this is the fire scrying of hearth and home or a garden bonfire. You can either look for these images after the initial observation of the nature of the flames or make them the entire focus of your fire scrying.

Because the fire is moving, you will see moving images, and one may rapidly change into another and then into another if you gaze at the center of the fire for several minutes. This form of scrying is very effective when you are relaxed and sleepy.

Before beginning, acknowledge the guardians of your home if you are working indoors. Also, whether you are indoors or out, call on the family ancestors for advice, who themselves sat by the fire over the centuries and, similar to you, hoped and dreamed in the firelight. Some people believe their essences gather at the family hearth on special occasions and bring blessings to the home.

Cast a few herbs or petals on the fire (leave the glass door of a stove open for a minute or two), and either formulate a question or ask to be shown what will best give you wise guidance in the days ahead. Answers may come as words in your head or more subtle feelings or impressions, as well as pictures.

If a friend or family member needs advice, or you are working with family or a partner on a joint issue, ask him or her to cast a handful of herbs in the fire and then to hold a stick in the flames, being careful that it only chars, while asking the question. Then they should cast the smoldering stick into the flames and, where it flares in the fire, an image will appear.

Ask the person to name the picture he or she sees in the fire or words and images that come into the mind without pausing to rationalize. You can then add what you see. This will continue to be the area of the fire where the joint images will appear and, as with individual divination, one may change into the other. Continue until four or five images have been obtained.

You can then both consider how the symbols together provide a solution to the questions or offer suggestions for moving on with life.

You can adapt the ritual using a large candle and a long incense stick that you can light from the candle as the question is asked. Hold the incense stick in the flame so it momentarily flares, and then leave it in a holder so the incense swirls in front of the candle adding to the visions. Sandalwood, myrrh, sage, and frankincense fragrances, rose petals, or any of the fire herbs listed earlier are especially potent for creating the relaxed state necessary for scrying for fire images.

Candle Scrying

Candle scrying is a perfect substitute for a fire if you live in a city and have central heating, though I would suggest to try open fire scrying when you can.

It is also a good way of connecting with angels, Spirit Guides, your distant ancestors, recently deceased relatives, or periods in history to which you feel spiritually connected.

Any white or beeswax candle is good for candle scrying, and the candle can be as large as you wish. Embed the candle in sand or earth in a large heatproof container or metal bucket. However, some people find it easier to scry with a tall, slender candle.

Unless you are also scrying with the wax (see Chapter 7), many people set the candle in a heatproof goblet such as a glass container. The whole candle, including the flame, should be within the glass so you get reflections on it.

You can also buy smaller fragranced candles that fill the glass container as opposed to standing separately within it. These types of candles diminish in size as the candle burns, so eventually you have a hollow of color with the wick near the bottom of the glass. These are good for scrying. Candles in glass are also effective for outdoor nighttime scrying as there is less risk of them going out, but the flames will still flicker. The fragrances help to relax the everyday consciousness. Short candles on a flat metal tray are ideal as you can tip the melting wax onto the metal dish. Work in darkness except for the light of the candle you are using.

Candle Colors

If you prefer, you can use specific colors that refer to particular areas of concern you are asking about. Alternatively, you can use your astrological zodiac color or that of a lover if you are asking about love or one to represent a family member

If you wish, engrave the Zodiacal glyph shown on pages 82 and 83 with a thin paper knife blade or metal nail (iron is traditional), or write a word on the candle to represent the question.

You can burn incense sticks or fragrance oils that are associated with the chosen color. You can shop around for the right color scented candles if you do not want to use incense. However, incense smoke curling around the candle also creates images.

You can also sprinkle just a few grains of the appropriate dried herbs or powder incense (the kind without resin) into the flame. Some fragrances and qualities or areas of concern belong to more than one color.

You can apply the following color meanings when you are setting up any other form of scrying that involves candles (for example, wax on water, general water scrying, or in crystals sphere or mirror work where candles provide light).

    ≫ **White:** New beginnings, health questions, original ideas and inventions, ambitions and success, Guardian Angels, life-changing issues, healing, the quest for what is of worth, strongly held desires and wishes, religious questions, fire scrying, and any issue under question. **Fragrances:** Bay (laurel) carnation, chamomile, heather, frankincense, juniper, rosemary, sagebrush.

❧ **Red:** Taking action, survival issues, changes, courage, physical strength and energy levels, passion, campaigns and crusades, sports, The Armed and Security Forces, adolescents and young men up to 30, and fire scrying. **Fragrances:** Basil, cinnamon, dragon's blood, ginger, hibiscus, mint.

❧ **Orange:** Confidence and self-esteem, matters of personal happiness, creativity, including writing, art, the arts, music, dance, independence and personal identity, the media, originality, abundance, fertility, balance, the workplace, self-employment, and female adolescents and young women up to 30. **Fragrances:** Juniper, marigold, neroli (orange blossom), orange, Saint-John's wort.

❧ **Yellow:** Logic and the mind, knowledge of all kinds and study, tests and examinations, business acumen, communication, technology and science, short-term or local travel, house moves, speculation, gambling, loans and credit matters, discovering the truth/honesty, and surgery and conventional medicine. **Fragrances:** Dill, eglantine or sweet briar, fennel, fern, fuchsia, lavender, lemongrass, tarragon.

❧ **Green:** Love, fidelity, harmony, good luck, gradual increase of money, environment, horticulture, forestry and herbalism, beauty and sexuality, altruism, gradual healing and recovery after illness, especially through alternative methods, mature women, all who love whatever their age or sex, communication with power animals and nature spirits, and earth scrying. **Fragrances:** Apple blossom, feverfew, geranium, cat mint, lily, rose, vanilla, violet.

❧ **Blue:** Ideals and principles, expansion of both perspective and physical horizons, leadership and authority, justice, career and promotion, long-term

or long-distance travel, house moves involving relocation or moving abroad or to another state, success,
marriage and business partnerships, mature men, any
scrying (especially air and water), and contacting
Water Guardians. **Fragrances:** Cedar, fig, honeysuckle, hyssop, meadowsweet, pine, sage, sandalwood.

- **Purple:** Contacting Spirit Guides, psychic development, contacting the ancestors, psychic protection,
spirituality, mediumship and the family deceased,
dream work, inner peace, past lives and unconscious
wisdom, healing of the mind and emotions, ancient
wisdom, astral travel, any scrying, retired people, and
wise women. **Fragrances:** Cypress, hyacinth, lemon
verbena, mimosa, mugwort, patchouli.

- **Pink:** Unconditional love, reconciliation, gentleness,
the mending of quarrels, patience, children and the
vulnerable, abuse, addictions and obsessions, the family, and pets. **Fragrances:** Cherry blossom, elder,
lilac, magnolia, peach, rose, strawberry.

- **Brown:** Nurturing issues, acceptance of frailty in
self and others, property and DIY, official organiza-
tions, banks and finance, animals, agriculture, contacting Earth Guardians and spirits who protect the
home, older people, protection of all kinds, chronic
illness, and pain. **Fragrances:** Cypress, ivy, lemon
balm, patchouli, saffron, sweetgrass, vetivert.

- **Black:** Some people do not like scrying with black
candles because of its associations with death and
bad spirits; however, in ncient Egypt it is the color
of rebirth, linked with the rich silt left by the Nile
Flood. It is also the color of the Chinese yin and
so the necessary polarity to white. However, if you
are not comfortable with scrying with it substitute
indigo, dark purple, or deep blue.

Endings, transitions, regeneration, acceptance of life as it is, confrontation of mortality, banishing anything from addictions to destructive people from your life, depression, grief and loss, the wise ancestors and more recent family deceased, and mediumship. **Fragrances:** cedar, juniper, lily of the valley, pine, sagebrush, sweetgrass, and thyme.

Gray: Compromises, adaptability, merging into the background or maintain a low profile, secrets, psychic protection, dark mirror, dark crystal, shadow and smoke scrying, talking to the wise ones who rule time, past lives, the reduction of anger, grief or guilt, and pain both emotional and physical. **Fragrances:** Almond, cumin, fern, lily of the valley, parsley, peppermint, rosemary, thyme.

Silver: Intuition, understanding dreams, hidden potential, fertility, conception, pregnancy, mothers and babies, mirror work, female cycles, the cycle of the year and the seasons, connection with sea, moon and star guardians, future lives and what is yet unknown, other dimensions (especially higher ones), moonlight scrying, water scrying (also blue), angel work, The Goddess, and mediumship and the deceased, especially mothers and grandmothers. **Fragrances:** Clary sage, eucalyptus, gardenia, jasmine, lemon, orchid, myrrh, poppy (opium), wintergreen.

Gold: Wealth and lasting prosperity, aiming high, great good fortune, perfection, wishes coming true, Sun and light beings and Guardians, all fathers, The God, spiritual healing, crystal sphere scrying, contacting Archangels and the highest dimensions, sunlight scrying, and fire scrying. **Fragrances:** Benzoin, copal, dragon's blood, frankincense, orange, sandalwood.

Astrological Colors

You can use these to represent yourself or others concerned in the question, with or without the zodiacal glyph on the side.

For each I have given a keyword to say or think as you light the candle; this helps you tune in with the zodiacal energies. You can light the fragrance of the zodiacal sign or add it as herbs or petals to the flame.

♈ **Aries,** the Ram (March 21st–April 20th)
Color: Red
Keyword: Action
Fragrance: Ginger or dragon's blood

♉ **Taurus,** the Bull (April 21st–May 21st)
Color: Pink
Keyword: Beauty
Fragrance: Apple blossom or rose

♊ **Gemini,** the Heavenly Twins (May 22nd–June 21st)
Color: Yellow
Keyword: Communication
Fragrance: Fennel or lemongrass

♋ **Cancer,** the Crab (June 22nd–July 22nd)
Color: Silver
Keyword: Sensitivity
Fragrance: Jasmine or poppy (opium)

♌ **Leo,** the Lion (July 23rd–August 23rd)
Color: Gold
Keyword: Leadership
Fragrance: Copal or frankincense

♍ **Virgo,** the Maiden (August 24th–September 22nd)
Color: Green
Keyword: Perfection
Fragrance: Lavender or lily of the valley

♎ **Libra,** the Scales (September 23rd–October 23rd)
  Color: Blue
  Keyword: Harmony
  Fragrance: Geranium or cat mint

♏ **Scorpio,** the Scorpion (October 24th–November 22nd)
  Color: Indigo or burgundy
  Keyword: Intensity
  Fragrance: Basil or cinnamon

♐ **Sagittarius,** the Archer (November 23rd–December 21st)
  Color: Orange or turquoise
  Keyword: Expansiveness
  Fragrance: Sage or sandalwood

♑ **Capricorn**, the Goat (December 22nd–January 22nd)
  Color: Brown
  Keyword: Wise caution
  Fragrance: Mimosa or patchouli

♒ **Aquarius,** the Water Carrier (January 21st–February 18th)
  Color: Purple
  Keyword: Idealism
  Fragrance: Lemonbalm/Melissa or thyme

♓ **Pisces**, the Fish (February 19th–March 20)
  Color: White or lilac
  Keyword: Intuition
  Fragrance: Honeysuckle or lemon

Practicing Candle Scrying

Choose your candle and any appropriate fragrance you wish to burn as incense or oil, or use a scented candle. In the chapter on dark mirror scrying we will look at candles reflected in a mirror. One candle is best for scrying especially at first. If it is a joint question or you are helping someone else, sit close and look at the same candle.

Light your candle with a taper (you can buy very thin wand-like wax candles or use long cook's matches) then the incense from the candle. Have no other light.

Ask that the Guardians of Fire and Light (see Chapter 1) or your Guardian Angel/Spirit Guides will protect you and show you what you most need to see. You can either ask a specific question aloud or accept whatever appears. You may find it helpful to say, "I am (give your first name) and I seek (ask question or add) whatever wisdom will best guide me (or name person for whom you are asking) in the days ahead."

The statement of I *am* and your name is a good way of centering yourself. Also it helps if you lack confidence of establishing your identity and your right/ability to find happiness (which deep down we sometimes doubt).

Though I previously suggested that you can make interpretations from the flame in the fire scrying section, on a whole candle scrying is best for seeing images. If you have a slight breeze, either with a partly opened window or a small fan, or if you are outdoors, the flickering flame may help you to focus. But avoid strong breezes.

Relax your eyes as if you were sleepy and let images form in and around the candle flame. If this is hard to do, focus on the flame, gently inhale the image of the candle light, seeing golden light entering you. Blow out softly through your mouth, similar to a sigh, so the golden light forms a sphere of light around the candle in your mind.

Continue inhaling and exhaling, making the sphere larger so that the candle flame becomes a large sphere of light where images can appear either in the candle image in your mind or the physical candle. For some people they always work within their mind's vision but the results are just as accurate. However, it is quite exciting to see the images physically around the candle. In time, you may be able to project the light so the actual candle flame looks much larger externally and the inner wick forms a doorway for connecting with angels or past worlds.

Let the images build up as you relax or, if you are still find-ing it hard, stare at the physical candle, close your eyes, open them slowly, blink, and *see* the image flash in front of you. At first the images may be fleeting either way, but in time and with practice you can sustain them for a minute or two. If you do lose the image, close your eyes and let it re-form in the light sphere in your mind.

Images tend to be different shades of red or orange, but yours may be black outlines. The images almost always move and flicker, even if the flame is still and tend to be two-dimensional. Relax, and when the image fades wait and see if another appears. Continue until you sense the connection fading. When you blow it out, look for a final message in the rising smoke, which may only last for a few seconds.

Also important are any messages you hear and any impres-sions/sensations that occur. If working to help someone else on a joint issue, name the images each of you sees and try to tune into the other person's image (seeing through his or her eyes) and add to it.

When you have finished, add another pinch of salt to the flame with thanks, and, if you have time, leave the candle to burn through, lighting others so you can work on the meanings in your scrying journal. If you have to go, blow out the light and send it to whoever needs it most.

This is an excellent way of communicating with a Guardian Angel, Spirit Guide, or departed loved one for advice or reassur-ance. Instead of saying, "I am," name the angel/guide or ances-tor/deceased relative you would wish to connect with. Breathe as before, allowing the image to appear around the enlarged flame or use the center of the flame around the wick as a door-way through which the spirit or guardian can walk. You can also use this doorway to glimpse a past world or another dimension if you hold your gaze steady.

Chapter 5

Scrying With Air

You do not need elaborate equipment to scry with Air. If we listen, Nature has provided us with a repository of wisdom in the wind, trees, and clouds.

What you need most is the hardest thing of all for humans: a time of stillness and inaction. It involves waiting to receive wisdom fresh on the wind, on how to move forward in new, fresh, revitalizing ways.

Whenever you feel stagnant, blocked by life or locked in old patterns, Air scrying will provide the impetus and confidence for positive change.

What do you need for Air scrying? Your eyes, your ears, and a willingness not to be blown off course, but rather gently pushed in the right direction.

In this chapter there are no tools to be cleansed, no equipment to be empowered. Mother Nature has taken care of all that.

Go into the open air, on your balcony, in your garden, a park or green space, or out in the countryside even, if for only a day. Whatever the weather, children will run free in the woods, by the sea, or on hillsides. And after the initial sulking, whatever their age they will build tree houses and find flowers or dig in the sand, collecting stones and shells as people have done for thousands of years. You can listen to and observe the messages of the Air undisturbed.

In Chapter 6 we will work with the sand, the earth, and the soil, but for now we are going to look upwards and all around us for inspiration. You may also receive insights from the nature essences, the angels of nature and the wise devas, and the higher nature beings akin to angels, who see that the blueprint of nature follows its appointed course.

Cloud Scrying

From the beginning of time, people have looked up at the clouds and the sky for messages and signs of favor from the deities. Rainbow, wind, and storm scrying are still practiced by indigenous people such as the Maori of New Zealand and in parts of sub-Saharan Africa whose culture and customs date back thousands of years.

Cloud scrying was one of the main forms of divination used by the Celtic Druid priests and priestesses who revered the sky, along with earth and sea, as the three sacred realms that held their counterparts in the spiritual world.

The Romans, too, believed in the prophetic power of clouds, not just for the shapes of the clouds that formed symbols and images, but as a source of actual visions. Most famous is the recorded case in 312 C.E. Emperor Constantine was marching against the army of Maxentius in Rome when he and his entire army saw a shining cross of light in the clouds and the words "By This Sign Conquer" written in Greek in the sky. That night, Constantine saw Jesus in a dream. Jesus was carrying a cross and told Constantine that he must ride out into battle with the Christian cross on his flag. Constantine did so and, though his army was far outnumbered, he won the battle.

Images of angels, doves of peace, and the Virgin Mary have often been seen in the clouds, especially at sunset. Certain places of natural beauty, such as mountaintops, have become famous for these sightings. St. Brynach, the Irish-born Celtic monk, used to regularly climb the Hill of the Angels above Nevern near Tenby in South West Wales to talk to the angels.

At Medjugorje, a small village in the former Yugoslavia, the Virgin Mary began appearing to six young people from the village: Ivan, Jakov, Marija, Mirjana, Vicka, and Ivanka. These six young people began having apparitions of the Blessed Virgin Mary on June 24, 1981, and wondrous events still occur at the pilgrimage site.

From that time on to the present day, manifestations of light that assume many forms have appeared in the sky. The first of these sky signs was seen on June 27, 1981. On that day, the Virgin Mary's coming was preceded by a brilliant light that illuminated not only the village, but the entire area, and was seen by everyone in the village. On June 28, 1981, a crowd of people gathered on Mount Podbrdo and witnessed again the light that immediately preceded the Virgin Mary's visitation to the six young visionaries.

The sign observed by the crowd on August 2, 1981, has been described as the "dancing of the sun." At the end of the event, a white cloud was seen coming down over the mountainside. It moved toward the sun, which continued to spin briefly, and then returned to its normal state. The entire phenomenon lasted about 15 minutes.

One of the most important aerial symbols that have been observed is the word *mir* (meaning *peace* in Croatian), which was written one evening in large, bright, burning letters in the sky above the Cross on Mount Krizevac. This particular sign has been observed numerous times between 1991–1995, and various other times, by the pastor and people from the village during the recent war in the region. The village escaped damage from the war in Croatia although all the surrounding area was affected.

Cloud Angels in the Sunset

Certain places in the natural world similar to those I previously described have become associated with angelic visitations and sightings or those of other religious or spiritual icons. Such visions may be experienced by different people at the same spot over many years. However, many ordinary people see angels in the clouds, at times such as sunset, from hills or mountaintops, on planes, or while standing in a room on a high floor of a hotel, apartment blocks, or offices.

Figures in the sky tend to be spontaneous and though they are most common before sunset, they may also appear in the daytime when the sun causes shafts of light to radiate in the sky.

Sky angels cannot be explained away purely as meteorological phenomena because they are far clearer than ordinary cloud images and fade quite suddenly and dramatically. They may be seen by a number of people at the same time and may flood the whole sky with a momentary brilliance.

Angelic cloud pictures are different in quality and intensity from other cloud images. From the e-mails I receive from individuals who consider their sky angel of sufficient importance, I have noticed that people usually notice them in the sunset or sunlit sky when they most need guidance or reassurance.

Observing Cloud Angels

If at all possible, stop when the vision appears and watch your angel or spiritual vision until it suddenly fades, which may last for several minutes.

Try to memorize any distinguishing features, as you may be able to subsequently identify your sky angel. Of course, it is no less special if you cannot. But Archangels particularly may be identifiable by what they are holding. For example, Michael, Archangel of the Sun, is pictured with golden wings in red and gold armor with a sword, a shield, and a date branch, and carrying the scales of justice or a white banner with a red cross. Raphael, the Archangel of Healing and Travelers, carries a tall staff. Gabriel, who rules over the sunset as well as the moon, has a golden horn, a white lily, or a lantern in his right hand, and with a mirror made of jasper in his left. (Look in the Useful Reading section for books on angels or go online to find out more.)

When the image has faded, scribble down the main features of what you saw. Note also what impressions you received about the angel and how the angel might be relevant to you, such as *female, an angel who cares for service personnel, an angel who seemed to be singing,* and so on. It may be that as you look at your angel, a name comes into to your mind that you can check in a book on angelology or online.

Finally, ask the angel if there is a message for you, or if their presence is a sign of blessing, even if you feel distinctly unloved.

You may discover on checking your diary that the sky angel appeared on the anniversary of a loved one's death, and so the message may take on personal significance.

Would other people seeing the angel receive the same name if they asked? It may be, as suggested from my own research, that each person perceives the angel in the unique way they most need to connect with it rather than having the same exact vision as someone else. This is no different from when two or three of you look at the same shape made by oil on water, which forms a unique image, filtered through each person's own psyche.

If you do witness a cloud angel with other people, ask them to draw what they saw, plus any impressions and names. A very closely knit group may have clairvoyantly scryed remarkably similar information from the vision.

Usually messages from cloud angels are about reconciliation and acceptance. Therefore, earthly help or support from an unexpected source should follow a few days after the vision. If you feel you need more input into the experience, light a gold or silver candle along with angelic incense in any floral fragrance, especially rose, violet, or carnation.

Look into the flame and picture the angel you saw within the flame or in your mind's vision. You may recall other details or impressions and, as a result, find it easier to connect with angelic energies and your own Guardian Angel.

How to Scry With Clouds

If you decide to use clouds for scrying as opposed to waiting for visions, the results will generally be less dramatic unless you are extremely fortunate.

As long as you have gaps between clouds, even banks of dark clouds with light on them can be used.

Sometimes you will be driving along and see the perfect cloud formation for scrying. For these moments, if you have time, park the car. It helps to keep a blanket in the back of the car so you can sit on the grass and watch the clouds comfortably. If necessary, you can read the sky quickly through the office window for instant input. Where possible, however, on a good weather day, make an occasion of your cloud scrying, especially studying slow moving clouds.

The best kinds of clouds for scrying are either the high, thin, wispy cirrus clouds that can appear in fabulous colors when the sun is low on the horizon, or the lower, fluffy, fair-weather cumulus clouds seen against a blue sky.

There are many other cloud conditions that may only last a relatively short time that can also be used for sky scrying.

The Changing Sky

Though you can ask absolutely any question at any time while cloud scrying, certain cloud formations have traditionally become associated with wisdom for particular purposes. They include:

‽ **Dawn:** For questions of new beginnings, new love, and creative ventures.

‽ **Storm clouds:** For changes you desire or need, justice, and confrontations.

‽ **Clouds reflected in the sea on sunny days:** For all emotional matters, fertility, and relationships.

‽ **Fluffy clouds in a blue sky:** For health, happiness, family matters, pets, and career.

‽ **Sunlit clouds:** For fertility, children, all artistic ventures, fame, and fortune.

‽ **Snow clouds:** For reconciliation, natural transitions and endings, protection, and transformation.

‽ **Fast-moving clouds:** For sudden opportunities, travel, house moves, the clearing of stagnation, or obstacles.

‽ **Rain clouds tinged by sun:** For money matters, healing, the revival or renewal of what you fear may be gone, questions about betrayal, and how to move on.

‽ **Small black clouds in an otherwise clear sky:** For irritating disputes between family members, work colleagues, or neighbors; addictions or problems with food, alcohol, or smoking that bother you.

‽ **Sunset clouds:** For angels and all spiritual matters and healing.

‽ **White or silver tinged clouds in the night sky:** For secrets to be revealed, finding what is lost, or news about those who are far away or estranged.

‽ **Moonlit clouds hiding the moon:** For secret love, unrequited love, finding a soul mate, and hidden fears.

Beginning Scrying

Before you begin asking questions, spend time cloud watching in different locations and at different times. While you are tuning into clouds, do not force pictures to form, but note any cloud formations that seem especially significant, and the feelings they evoke. Above all, do not hurry the experience. The essence is a calm, still frame of mind when you are not clock watching or fretting about unfinished tasks.

Asking Questions of the Skies

Find an open place, such as a hilltop or open field, at a time when the clouds overhead are sufficiently separate to make individual images.

Begin by making a connection with the guardian devas of the place where you are cloud watching; ask their permission and to aid your insights. You do not need to know their names—just sense their presence, which may manifest as shimmers of light and shadow or as tall misty or shadowy pillars that form and reform and are constantly moving.

Connect with the clouds, breathing gently and regularly. From your mind, allow any free-floating thoughts or anxieties to float away on the clouds. This interim period can be helpful if you lead a busy life or are very logical-minded. Picture your energy field merging with the grass and the sky so that you breathe as one in time with the pulse of nature.

Allow a question to emerge quite naturally and softly say it aloud, blowing gently between each word.

Then, sit or lay so you are totally comfortable, half-close your eyes, and let the images float above you. A single cloud may create an image, or two or more clouds may seem closely connected as a single idea (for example, a cat chasing a bird who is constantly hopping or flying just out of the pouncing cat's claws as one cloud pursues the other across the sky).

For each image or idea, extract as much information as possible. For example, if you see a cloud dragon is it fire breathing and fierce? An Air dragon scattering the seeds of new life or bringing rain? An Earth dragon guarding treasure? Who does the dragon represent in your life? What message does the dragon have for you?

Of course, if the clouds are moving fast, all these insights may be quite instantaneous, and that will prevent your logical mind from intruding. But other times when clouds are slow-moving, you can contemplate at your leisure.

After each image or related set of images, scribble a rough drawing and keywords in a notebook. You can contemplate these further when you have collected all of your images. Wait while the clouds move on, and reform, and continue until you have at least five or six images relating to the question.

If another question emerges spontaneously, you can answer it in the same way, collecting from the clouds a further series of images. Otherwise, thank the guardian devas for the use of the place, bury a small coin in the earth, and sit quietly for a while longer watching the clouds, but without making any conscious images or connections. Walk home or back to your car slowly, by which time the conscious mind will have joined with the psyche to make even more connections and meanings.

Before dark or by white candlelight, copy the relevant material into your scrying journal, and, if the connections are still elusive, weave a story around the images and messages with yourself as the hero or heroine. You might prefer to write a poem (it does not have to rhyme) or paint a picture.

Before going to sleep, look up at the night sky and ask that the wisdom you gained will be expanded in your dreams. Close your eyes in bed and picture either the fluffy clouds in the blue sky or the stars as you drift into sleep.

Collective Cloud Work

Cloud scrying with others can be immensely rewarding as a group activity or with two or three trusted friends, family members, or a partner to resolve relationship issues creatively.

Collective cloud work is also a good way of planning a strategy for a joint venture or activity. You will need a cassette recorder, as there will be a lot of material to remember. Briefly explain the technique in advance if others are unfamiliar with it.

Sit on a hilltop or in an open place. Everyone should face the same bank of clouds in a pre-decided area of the sky. As before, greet the guardians of the place, perhaps each one of you making a greeting in turn.

Sit in silence tuning into the clouds. You need not decide upon a question unless there is a collective decision to be made; you can leave the scrying open to inspiration.

Choose one person in advance to begin the cloud observation and remember to keep talking until all the inspiration has been expressed. The first person identifies a cloud (for example, "I see a lioness."). Do not be afraid to express emotions and impressions and, where possible, set the image in its context, (such as, "The lioness is leaving the forest and entering a clearing. She knows she must find other lions to survive the coming winter.")

When the first person has finished, the next person picks another cloud. Their scene may be connected, but often the link is not at first clear. "I see a wolf. He has lost the pack because he is running from the hunters. But he feels no regrets as the others were too slow. He is a lone wolf by nature."

If working with a partner you can alternate choosing images and tune into each other's visions so you see the same image and perhaps expand on it.

When you have finished, play the recording; listen in silence. Then discuss the ideas between you and see how they all connect, and how any obvious differences might be reconciled.

Perhaps the cloud impressions symbolize a situation in the world arena, a concern you all have for a local issue or one that mirrors the uncertainties and decisions you are all struggling with. The wolf and the lioness, for example, are moving in opposite directions, the lioness seeking others, the wolf leaving. Which would need to happen first? Could both happen without damage to the other? What linking images can resolve the needs of two people with opposite viewpoints or priorities. Did any unexpected factors emerge?

When you are alone, as with your personal cloud work, expand on the story, perhaps in verse, painting the images or sculpting the cloud characters. You may enter the scene in your dreams where the landscape will expand. You can take these insights back to the group, family, or partner.

The Power of the Wind

The wind has many voices, from wild shrieks during a storm over the sea, the howl as it rushes between tall narrow buildings, the fury of a tornado or whirlwind, the hum in the sails of a yacht on a choppy sea, to the melodious song of a grove of trees swaying in harmony in a gentle breeze.

An old superstition in Wales says that if you stand at a crossroads at midnight on Halloween, the wind will tell you all you need to know about the coming year.

In Greek and Roman myth, the four winds were given names and personalities. In the myths, there were four brothers, sons of Eos, father of the winds, and Aurora, the goddess of the dawn. They lived on the floating island of Aiolia. He released the winds on instructions of the deities.

The North Wind

Boreas was the North Wind. He had brown wings, a dragon's tail, a rain cloud cloak, and streaming white hair, and was very tempestuous.

You can ask the North wind questions about endings in your life, about the past and past worlds, about your security, property, and financial security, about chronic illnesses or pain, older people, animals of all kinds, fears, and bad habits.

Talk about these worries with him or any other cold wind blowing from a different direction that swirls snow or hail, whips up the seas to give foam images, or howls on cold dark nights through passageways.

His message: Cast away what is no longer of value or has ceased to give you joy, but embrace what is of worth.

The East Wind

Apheliotes (Eurus in Latin) rules the East wind. He was the youngest of the brothers and was always impatient to be away, flying through the sky scattering clouds.

You can ask the East wind questions about new beginnings, new love, any changes in direction in your life, travel, new activities, or business—especially self employment, career moves or new homes, health worries, and obstacles or stagnation that hold you back.

Talk about these worries with him or to any other wind that blows in swirling rain squalls, shakes the blossoms from the trees creating pictures and patterns you, and creates sky pictures as birds swoop and dive while making their nests. Listen also to the bird song and calls for clairaudient messages.

His message: Change what is necessary for fulfillment, but do not embrace change for change's sake.

The South Wind

Notus rules the South wind. He is the most amiable of the winds, filled with sunlight and emitting sparkling light beams in his wake.

You can ask the South wind about prosperity, about expansion in career or personal growth, about fertility, commitment, and fidelity, about worries about acute illnesses, and to predict good luck and bring good news.

Talk about these with him and with any other wind that blows the long grasses or crops creating patterns, shakes the leaves melodiously in a grove of trees, or lifts the sand to make heaps and shapes (see also Chapter 8 for sand reading).

His message: Enjoy today and do not worry about tomorrow or yesterday.

The West Wind

Zephyrus rules the West wind. He is a gentle wind, is married to Iris, goddess of the rainbow, and fills the sails of boats with breezes when they become still.

You can ask the West wind about justice, peace and reconciliation, reaping the rewards of earlier work or input, debt worries, love in later years or remarriage and step-families, and healing old sorrows.

Talk about these with him or any wind that makes pictures by blowing the petals off dying flowers, tosses autumn leaves, or brings swirling mists through which the sun breaks to form golden images.

His message: Forgive what cannot be put right, and, most of all, forgive yourself.

Wind Scrying

Ancient Greeks practiced wind scrying in the sacred grove of oak trees at Dodona, which was dedicated to their father, Zeus.

Here, wooden wands were hung from the trees so that when the wind blew they banged against brass bowls also suspended from the trees. The resulting sounds were interpreted by the priestesses who lived in the grove.

The musical sounds triggered off not only words, but visions in the minds of the priestesses, both to answer questions from seekers at the grove and also to make prophecies about future events. Wind scrying does not always need trees, as I have previously suggested.

But the combination of wind and leaves brings a very special spiritual intensity. You do not have to believe in actual tree spirits, who have featured in almost every culture, the devas of nature to work with the trees. However, trees do undoubtedly have power-ful animate energies that have been described as these mythical, or maybe actual, personalities of tree essences or spirits.

The Life Within the Trees

For wind scrying with leaves, you may find it helpful to picture these creatures within the moving patterns of the tree. You can also to ask a wise deva, described as a tall, green-robed opalescent being, to help you see and hear the messages of the wind in the trees.

Nature spirits from the Celtic, European, Mediterranean, and Scandinavian traditions seem, as did the widely reported banshee or family spirit, to have travelled with early settlers to the Americas and the southern hemisphere, settling alongside the folk lore of indigenous spirits. Therefore, wherever you live you can work with these older tree spirit personas as well as with indigenous spirits. They include:

Bokwus

A native North American male spirit found near rushing water in North American spruce forests.

Cururipur

A South American spirit of rainforest and jungle who is guardian of wild creatures, especially tortoises.

Dryads

Female tree nymphs, so named in ancient Greece, also found in Celtic mythology. They are associated especially with willow, the tree of the moon, and with oak and ash.

Gianes

Solitary Italian wood elves, famed for their skill in weaving and divination using the movement of their spinning wheels to create images.

Ghillie Dhu

Scottish tree spirits who live mainly in birch trees and hide in foliage to avoid observation.

Hamadryads/Hamadryadniks

Hamadryads are similar to dryads, but remain within the same tree, especially oak trees. They die if it is cut down, unless you can rescue a part of the root system and replant it fast.

Hamadryadniks are Eastern European tree spirits who disguise themselves as foliage; but unusually for tree spirits they leave their homes during daylight.

Hyldermoder

Scandinavian and Northern European tree mothers that live in elder trees, the most magical of all fairy plants.

The term can also be applied to the tree women of any other species whose face you can see in the trunk and whose form and voice appear in the moving leaves.

Lunantishess/Lunantisidhe

Irish blackthorn fairies. The blackthorn fairies worship the Moon Goddess and love the winter.

Moss Wives or Wood Wives

Wood or moss wives, gentle and helpful female tree spirits, found especially in Germany and the Netherlands. Moss wives live on even if the tree dies.

Nemetona or Nemain

Celtic Mother of the sacred groves and forests who may speak through the rustling leaves of any tree, or whose form may suddenly appear momentarily as the wind lifts and scatters a pile of autumn leaves.

Radande

Powerful higher Scandinavian tree spirits, akin to devas, who watch over the management of forests by humans and give protection to forests and all the creatures that live in them.

Skogara

Also called the wood nymph or Huldra in Sweden, a more glamorous tree spirit except when she shapeshifts into a hag. Usually she is pictured as a single spirit, called Skogs Fru in Norway. She can become a whirlwind if angry.

Tengu

Japanese-winged woodland fairies who carry fans made of feathers, and who may take on the shape of woodland animals.

Wind Scrying With the Trees

A tree is the wind's palette of paints, and, if you watch on a windy day, it will create pictures for you. These pictures are made from the changing patterns of the leaves, the moving branches, and the spaces between them through which you can see the sky as the wind blows.

The sound of the wind blowing the trees speaks messages as you become used to the sound patterns of different intensities and the sound of the wind blowing through different kinds of trees. The voice of the pine or redwood forest is very different from the sound of a grove of statuesque oaks.

In addition, the sounds create strong visual pictures in the mind to expand those seen in the leaves. At this point whatever you were asking about is perfectly clear.

To amplify these effects, similar to the priestesses in the ancient oak groves of Dodona, you can hang wooden and metal wind chimes and bells from a tree in your garden or anywhere the wind can flow freely.

Beginning Wind and Leaf Scrying

To tune into the energies of the chosen place, you should, as with cloud scrying, acknowledge the spirit of the forest or grove.

Each forest or grove of trees has a higher spiritual energy or essence that a number of people describe as a deva. In human terms, that is akin to the managing director of a business.

The individual trees will have separate energies similar to those I described as the tree spirit types. Often you get one kind of tree spirit in an area of woodland. These energies tend to be expressed similar to any mortal group who live and work together every day, as an overall common aura or mood of the forest. If you do work with a single tree for scrying, you need to connect with the individual characteristic energy as well as that of its ruling deva.

You can of course look for images in the moving leaves and listen to the sound created by the wind without any reference to devas or tree spirits. If you do, use precisely the same technique as the one I suggest in the following pages.

However, by tuning into the energies of the prevailing wind and the group of trees you are working with, whether you regarded them as objective essences or personifications of those essences, you are able to receive much deeper insights. You can also draw strength from the higher wisdom of the nature devas (even if you regard this as a projection of your own higher self).

To me, scrying with trees as though they were inanimate tools, such as a bowl of water, is similar to going into someone's house without asking while they are sitting watching a movie, eating your dinner at their table while totally ignoring them, and then going off without a word.

Because oaks can live for more than a thousand years and yews for 2,000 years, they have seen many ages, many joys and sorrows, and so are good teachers, especially when you need to see issues into perspective.

Wind and Tree §crying

Begin by standing or sitting where there are a number of trees close together when it is windy. This could be in your garden, a park, or a forest. Gradually allow your mind to become attuned to the rhythm of the rise and fall of the sound of the wind and the rustling leaves, followed by a lull. Before long it will take on the pattern of whispered voices. Also watch the patterns made by the leaves on individual trees and the whole grove so that you become attuned to their movement.

When you feel ready, walk over and touch a tree that seems welcoming. Ask permission of its individual spirit and the deva of the forest to seek wisdom though its voices, and that the essences of the forest will protect you.

You may become aware of the presences of the individual tree spirits and of the deva, shadowy, tall, and constantly moving like the wind, with glimmers of green shimmering light, at sunrise or sunset tinged with gold, and in moonlight dressed in silver. There is nothing spooky about this; rather it a sense of being admitted to a sacred place of wisdom. The Druids used groves of trees as their temples.

Even the scruffiest urban park grove is a place of beauty beneath what the careless humans have done. If you choose an uncared for urban wood you can perhaps encourage a local initiative for replanting and clearing any trash.

Sit until a question comes spontaneously into your mind. Either speak it aloud or carve it with a knife on smooth, fallen wood and cast it as far as possible during the pause between wind gusts. If you have no specific question, let the breeze-blown leaves share their wisdom.

Look upwards and watch the leaves and branches come together and part, sway and move. The pictures they suggest are not similar to those that appear in water, oils, or even in a crystal sphere, but are formed of the greens and browns in different shades and densities. They are fleeting, similar to scenes flashing past the window while you are sitting on an express train, which imprint certain powerful features of the scenery in your mind. These might include a lake shimmering with ice, a brightly painted wooden house with a flag on top, or two horses racing in a field.

Even so, from your tree scenes you may recall one or two powerful images. Each time the tree is shaken, the picture will slowly form. As the intensity of the wind builds up, so the picture becomes stronger and more vivid, gradually slowing into silence as it fades.

When you have collected enough strong impressions for those pictures, close your eyes and listen to the words made by the leaves as they rustle. The sound of the leaves and the wind will intermingle as though a person was speaking to you.

The message is sometimes in verse or in a single phrase, followed by a lull, and may be completed in the next gust.

When the message is finished, wait in case there are any more words you need to hear. The pictures you saw in the leaves may flash vividly through your mind, adding fragrances, emotions, or impressions. If you wish to continue, take the time to allow further questions to evolve and be cast upon the wind.

Finally, touch the tree trunk of your special tree in thanks and let its strength and healing quiet disharmonious thoughts and renew your energy.

Leave an offering for the wild birds or small animals who live in or under in the tree. Scribble down any words, images, or impressions that came into your mind.

Developing Leaf and Wind Scrying

After you have been wind scrying on different occasions for some months, the whole experience will come together much faster and you will recall whole scenes vividly as though the train stopped for you at each of those vital vistas. You may even begin to perceive other dimensions of time as you watch the moving leaves.

As you become more experienced, too, the words of the winds and the leaves will tell you quite clearly either the path ahead or remind you of other dimensions, places, and ages that are right for you now.

Before long, you will begin to hear messages in other voices of nature, such as the rain beating on the roof or the crash of the sea against rocks.

You can visit other forests, palm trees around a desert oasis on vacation, a magnificent national park with huge redwoods, a eucalyptus grove, or a shimmering, snow-covered pine forest. Each will have its own devas and its own spirits, from whom you can gain different kinds of wisdom, rooted in the nature of the terrain.

Chapter 6

Earth Scrying

Watch a child on a beach or in a forest, arranging stones or shells in patterns, or pushing piles of sand with his or her hands to make towns, palaces, or magical kingdoms. Before you begin Earth scrying, take a day from your schedule to sit on the shore, a river bank, lakeside, or a forest clearing and recapture those moments. If you are with a partner or family member, make joint "worlds" in the sand, and, though you need not analyze them, a sense of easy companionship will grow that seem to iron out any minor irritations you brought with you in the relationship.

Earth divination is one of the oldest forms of divination. Early Shamans, priests, and healers predicted the future from patterns made in sand or earth, created by throwing down handfuls of pebbles, nuts, or seeds on to the ground. These readings were believed to reveal the will of the Earth Mother, expressed in the relationship between the stones, bones, or nuts cast, the earth on which they fell, and the intuition of the interpreter. Such practices continue today among hunting and fishing people whose lives have been relatively unchanged over the millennia.

Earth scrying is very instinctive, similar to Air scrying, needing very little in the way of external tools or preparatory rituals.

Earth scrying is dedicated to the Earth Mother, whether you view her as the Earth itself or personified in a goddess form. My own favorite Earth Mother is the Australian Aboriginal creator woman Warramurrungundjui, who emerged from the sea and gave birth to the first people. Warramurrungundjui, according to legend, carried a digging stick and a bag of food plants, medicinal plants, and flowers. Having planted them, she went on to dig the water holes. Then, leaving her children to enjoy the fruits of her work, she turned herself into a rock.

Scrying With Herbs

My own favorite Earth scrying method is using herbs, either cast on to a flat surface or floated on a bowl of water. I became interested in this art when I was training as a Druidess (a Nature priestess); during the second Ovate Grade, I explored scrying using traditional natural materials similar to herbs the Celts might have used.

The higher energy that I focused on for my Druidic herb scrying was the daughter of Mother Earth, Airmid, the Irish healing goddess of medicinal plants and herbs. The daughter of Diancect, the god of medicine, Airmid cared for the grave of her brother Miach and, on this, all the herbs of the world grew. As she cut them each described its healing properties. Myths tell how her father destroyed this knowledge and many of the herbs. This may be a symbolic reference to the appropriation of healing by male physicians in more patriarchal times.

Herb Scrying

The psychic eye perceives the clusters of herbs that are formed when they are scattered as images that relate to the matter under consideration. The images physically resembles an outline drawn by a child rather than a photographic image.

You can ask about any area of your life, but naturally herbs are particularly tuned into all domestic and family matters, such as health, animals, love, relationships, security of all kinds, and personal or family finances.

On a whole, you will get practical solutions, and it is not often you will see an angel, ancestor, or Guide, though past life scenes are possible. You can specify if you want to see a past scene, and these are most successful when floating herbs on water.

Choosing Your Herbs

You can use absolutely any dried herbs for scrying, the kind you buy in glass jars in the spices section of the supermarket. Parsley, sage, rosemary, and thyme, the four traditional divinatory herbs give clear images, as do chives, tarragon, and basil. Larger, distinct leaves are best, rather than powdered ones, which do not give such precise images.

If you frequently practice herb scrying as I do, you can grow, dry, and chop your own herbs. I have a scrying herb bed in my garden, but you can equally keep pots of scrying herbs on a balcony or on a sunny, dry window ledge. Kitchens can be too steamy for them to thrive.

Hang them upside down to dry, tied in bunches in a warm, dry spot where air can circulate until they become crumbly, but not brown. Store them in small, sealed glass jars.

Making Dried Herb Pictures

The simplest method is to use a flat, transparent glass chopping board or a light-colored round or rectangular wooden tray with shallow edges as the surface for the herbs. Make sure the surface is completely dry. You can alternatively cast the herbs on a very thick matte or a piece of white paper.

Work outdoors on a picnic table or on the ground, or indoors sitting at your kitchen or dining room table in sunshine.

You can work privately or informally with a partner, friend, or family member to help resolve his or her questions. It may be a helpful introductory method with a client who is new to psychic work and perhaps very nervous. For such sessions, I use a plain tablecloth rather than a more glitzy one, and serve coffee or juice and cookies during the session.

As for herb and water scrying, the dedication can be informal. I do not designate special tools but use an ordinary, everyday household chopping board, tray, or computer printer paper as long as it is totally clean. Apart from tea leaf or coffee grounds, this is the most homely of scrying arts, and domestic items make it feel much grounded.

Put your herbs ready in an open bowl on the table.

Before beginning you can sprinkle a little salt around the outside of the scrying surface you are using in a clockwise circle and/or silently ask for the blessings and protection of the Earth Mother (or Airmid, her daughter). If you wish, have four small potted herbs at the four corners on your table where they will not get in the way.

If working with another person, sit side by side so you can see the images from the same perspective.

Finding Answers

Ask a question or get the other person to formulate one. If you prefer, ask that you be shown what you most need to know at this time. Scatter just a small handful of herbs onto the scrying surface and shake the paper, tray, or chopping board very gently using both hands, so that the herbs form clusters but do not fall off.

You can add more herbs during the reading. You may get a number of separate images, or a picture or scene may suggest itself from the clusters of herbs. The images tend to be so obvious that you do not need to practice for dry herb scrying unless you want to.

If working with someone else, point out what you can see in the herbs and then ask what they see in the herb patterns. It may be entirely different and will give a new perspective. Discuss the findings, or if you're alone, scribble down on a separate piece of paper what you feel, and any words that come into your mind as you look at the picture or images. You can draw the images as well as using words.

Then if you feel you need more information, add another half handful of herbs to the scrying surface, and gently shake the herb formation to create a new picture or more images. This is similar to moving a kaleidoscope to change the patterns.

If working on behalf of someone else or answering a shared question, ask the other person to add the new herbs and to shake the tray. This time let him or her identify the new images/scene first. You can then add your interpretation. If working alone, scribble down your new impressions in words and pictures.

You can either get additional information about the original question or ask a new one. Continue to add herbs, though not too many, and reform the previous picture by shaking regularly.

When you feel that the session should end, tip the herbs into a large container that you can scatter outside later. Scatter a little salt over the scrying surface, silently thanking the Earth Mother or her daughter. You can dispose of the paper later in an environmentally friendly way.

Sit quietly and study what you wrote or drew, or discuss the conclusions with your client/family member.

Herbs on Water

This is only slightly more complicated. If you have not practiced dry herb scrying first, you may wish to float a handful of
herbs on the surface of a half-filled bowl of water and get used
to identifying the swirling images. Again, you can use the
method to answer your own questions or to help someone else.
With herb and water scrying, when using a very large bowl, you
can work with a number of people on a joint question or concern. Each will drop herbs on the water in turn, naming his or
her image with everyone interpreting them. Alternatively, you
can take it in turns to answer one another's questions, washing
out the bowl in between questions.

Use the same kinds of herbs as before, and choose a bowl
made of glass or white ceramic, either individual dessert-sized
or a larger one if more than one of you is working. I actually
prefer the larger bowl when working alone, but some people
feel a smaller bowl helps to concentrate the visions.

With either size, if the bowl becomes too full of herbs, you
can rinse it out and start again at any time during the reading
without interrupting the flow.

An ordinary household bowl rather than a special scrying bowl
is ideal, and you can dedicate it before the session by half-filling it
with water. Add a pinch of salt and swirl it clockwise, while silently
asking the blessings of Mother Earth or her daughter.

Rinse it out and refill with about half a bowl full from a tap
that has been running for a minute or two. Put the herbs nearby
in an open bowl. If more than one of you is working, you can sit
on either side of the bowl, as you will be studying it from all
angles.

Herb and water scrying are best in daylight. The sun should
not be reflected directly on the water. The secret of successful
herb and water scrying is adding a few herbs at a time. You will
soon get used to the correct amount.

After adding the herbs, either swirl the bowl several times, or stir the water with the index finger of the hand you write with or a clear crystal point clockwise.

Ask a question that you need answered.

Interpreting Images

At first, note any images that instantly appear. Remember: You are looking for impressions rather than photo-like representations. Keep naming the images rapidly one after the other, so that your logical mind does not intrude.

You may become aware that one image is larger and clearer than the others and appears almost immediately. This is often the heart of the answer and the other images will add information to this central theme. Some people see a whole scene suggested by the herbs, and you can interpret that as part of a reading. Focus on the whole scene and what seem to be major images within it.

Turn the bowl around in your hands or on the table as often as you like to study the images from all angles. Moving herbs are easiest for interpreting.

If you aren't seeing any recognisable shapes in the water, close your eyes, open them, blink, and say out loud what the image is. Your clairvoyant eye tends to be faster than the physical one for detecting symbols, but with practice they will soon move in sync.

Structuring the Reading

If you want to structure the clairvoyant information, ask before beginning that you be shown three images. Swirl the water around between images.

The first image will define the true issue or question, which may be very different from the one you thought you were asking. The second will tell you what the best action is or if inaction is better. The third will tell you the likely outcome of any action or inaction. If you wish, try for a fourth image to reveal what is unexpected.

Alternatively, structure the reading as a time line, designating the first image as revealing what factor or person from the past is of importance for the future. The second would indicate what present factor or person from the present will be of help for the future. The third is what may happen six months ahead. You can if you wish add images for a year and then five years ahead.

Basically, how your structure the reading is up to you, and your clairvoyant eye will use that structure to reveal the hidden information.

Stone and Sand Divination

Though I previously mentioned playing with sand and stones, these are in fact very old and mystical methods of divination. Some have been incorporated into complex systems such as African or stone or bone divination, common throughout sub-Saharan African cultures.

A system of Geomantic divination, interpreting stones cast on earth, came out of Africa and spread via Arabia to Europe during the early Middle Ages. Here, a new system came up, based on a grid formation and specific figures formed by patterns of dots. In Europe during the 19th century, Geomantic divination enjoyed a revival when it was developed as part of Napoleon's *Book of Fate*, although it has no connection with the general Napoleon. The members of the occult Order of the Golden Dawn adopted Geomantic practices during the early years of the 20th century.

An African version, Ifa, comes from the oracular tradition of the Yoruba people in south-west Nigeria. It spread to America with the slave trade and has formed a parallel tradition to the first one I mentioned. These formal systems of Earth divination, though well worth studying, are beyond the range of this book.

The Influence of the Middle East

A number of sand interpretation methods have passed from Egypt and Africa to Westernized traditions. But it is among the Bedouins, the nomadic peoples of the Middle East who have a strong presence in the deserts of Egypt, that sand and stone divination can still be seen most powerfully, practiced by their Fugara or Shamans. These Shamans are often synonymous in modern times with the man or wise woman of the village. But the wise grandmothers can also be seen outside the ornate tents casting stones on to sand for tourists and, more importantly, privately to answer family matters, using their own idiosyncratic versions.

In modern Egypt, especially in towns where the houses give way to the desert, such as Giza or Saqqara near Cairo, Bedouin families have now settled; the old traditions are handed down even among those of strong Muslim or Christian faith as part of their ancient heritage.

In old Bedouin tradition, the markings on the sand were, it was believed, created by an Elemental spirit. Also, the wise ancestors offered guidance and were asked to bring good fortune.

But in modern terms, we can view sand and stone divination as contacting the wise hidden part of ourselves. We all carry within ourselves the wisdom of the past in our genes and maybe in our deep memories, so in a sense every act of contemplation touches the world of our ancestors.

Sand reading is remarkably good for bringing to the surface any hidden aspects of your life, or events or opportunities that are hidden and have not moved on to the horizon. I have adapted it a little for modern urban westernized practice.

The Tools of Sand and Stone Divination

Work in soft shimmering sunlight, or on silver sand as the moon and stars are shining down, or when the light of dawn or sunset stains the earth different shades of scarlet, pink, orange, and purple. You will need:

- Seven small, smooth, round stones of similar size: six white and one red. Keep your stones when not in use in a drawstring bag.

- An enclosed circle of sand about 2 or 3 feet around, marked off by sand walls. You can also use a rectangular or square child's sandbox or a high-sided tray of similar dimensions. You can buy sandbox sand from any toy store. (Builder's sand can be too coarse and contain glass slivers). Alternatively, you can buy a range of colored sands and mix them in a large deep tray so that it is half full.

- You will also need a long, thin, dry stick from a sun tree such as palm, orange, lemon, bay, ash, laurel, or any fruit or nut-bearing tree.

Sand and Stone Scrying in Practice

Work alone where and when you will not be disturbed. If you are very emotionally close to someone or have a favorite long-term client, this can be a very intimate loving form of giving advice. You will need to carry out and interpret the processes while the person remains silent.

Sand scrying is enhanced by psychometry or psychic touch and passes information through your sensitive fingertips and palm chakra energy centers. The rhythm of your fingers through the sand induces a light trance state in which your unconscious wisdom can speak to you. Your unconscious wisdom will use the sand to express ideas that will be of use to you in future decision-making.

You can ask a question, but I find sand and stone work is best when you do not focus on anything specific, but allow the experience to unfold.

Unless you have an excellent memory, have a portable cassette recorder close by to record your insights as they flow. Speak aloud what you see, what you feel, and what you sense, as this is a very fluid and verbose form of scrying. Even if what you are saying does not seem to make sense, it will all fit together when you listen later.

If working on a beach, or in large sandpit or desert, mark the approximate limits of your divinatory area. Kneel or sit so you are above the sand. Before beginning, you can bless your sandbox and stone silently in the name of Nephthys, ancient Egyptian goddess of the desert, mysteries, and twilight who was called "lady of the desert, flower of barren places." Her special symbols were bright red desert flowers, so you can place a red flower in each corner of your sand while scrying if you wish.

Working With the Sand

Close your eyes and allow your hands to run through the sand, forming it into ridges and hills. When you are ready, open your eyes and gaze at the sandscape without consciously focusing on any issues. Switch on your recorder as the shimmering sand hills may evoke images or impressions. It may instantly suggest a scene or theme, a palace, a battleground, or a mass of people walking along a street. Go with this first spontaneous image and do not rationalize it, however unlikely, as that will set the framework for your scrying.

Allow words and images to form, and describe the scene aloud as though you were describing it to a friend. How does the scene make you feel? Happy, uneasy, regretful? Can you identify any characters in your sand scene or groups of people who are significant to any decision you/the client may be making?

Adding the Stones

Now between your cupped hands, hold the seven stones. Close your hands, shake them, and cast them downwards, so that they make a formation in the sand. Using the red stone as the marker, note how the stones are clustered. The cluster containing the red stone (or if it is alone, the area of the red stone), defines the hidden issue. If the stones are scattered there are a number of factors that will need to come together. Once you discover what they are from the divination, you can devise ways of hastening the integration. The more stones that are close to the marker stone, the more major and imminent the event or change.

If there are two or three distinct groups of stones, the future step forward may come slowly through smaller stages.

Using the Stones as a Gateway

Now close your eyes, open them, and stare at the main group containing the red stone, or the red stone if alone, set among the contours of the sand heaps.

Speak into the recorder what it is you see. Project yourself into a scene and make each of the stones part of the backdrop, whether as buildings into home, doorways into temples or workplaces, or even the past, where people will speak and show you events related to your own.

The scenes evoked by the stones may be a continuation of the original scene you saw before casting them or be the next stage or have changed into something completely different.

Go through all the other groups of stones or individual stones in the same way and finally close your eyes, open them, and stare at the whole scene in the sandbox for a final time. Once more, let the words come of what you feel and hear as well as see.

Only one stage remains. Taking the stick in your power hand, the one you write with, close your eyes and allow it to draw a large shape enclosing the stones. Allow the stick to move in and out, creating its own pathways. When you are finished, open your eyes, stare hard at the sand, and say, "Let me see in sand the message." Name without a pause what shape or animal you have drawn and, again without pausing to think, name its significance in your future life.

Replace the stones in the bag and erase the sand images so the sand is smooth again. Though the divination may seem to take hours, it is not usually longer than 30 minutes.

The scene may have been in no way related to sand and deserts, but bustling towns or even a crowded modern city in winter. It may have been entirely related to a past world you once knew. Each divination is different, exciting, and very tiring, so only do it monthly.

In the evening, light orange, lotus, or cedar essential oil or incense and an orange- or red-colored candle. Replay the tape and let the ideas fall into place. Draw up an action plan in your mind to make future positive events come into your life when the time is right, based on the uncovered wisdom.

Rock Sculptures

Many natural rock formations on cliffs, mountainsides, or rocky areas of land have natural faces or figure formations within them. As a result the rock may be named after a giant, a troll, or some local deity.

One example is the "Sleeping Beauty" (also known as the "Sleeping Mother" or "Sleeping Goddess") on the island of Lewis in the Outer Hebrides off the west coast of Scotland. The mountain appears to be a sleeping goddess when it is seen from a local stone circle, and in legend is said to be the home of the winged sylph Air spirits. Every 18 1/2 years the moon appears to be born from the Goddess figure.

You may have your own local rocks or cliff faces where you can see figures and formations. When you see faces or forms in rocks in other places you visit, you may afterwards find a local legend that confirms what you saw.

Although these are not scrying places per se, if you focus on the face you will often hear messages in your mind, reminding you of an old dream or gift you have laid aside.

Over time, if you visit the same place, the face or form will become a guide to you. And if you close your eyes, you will see pictures in your mind that will offer an unconsidered option. I often talk to the bearded Roman in the cliffs at the foot of the steep path near my holiday trailer.

Chapter 7

Scrying With Wax

In Chapter 4, I described how you could scry with a candle by observing the effects of the images evoked by the candle flame. Wax scrying is often combined with candle flame scrying but, because it is an art in itself, I have described it separately.

Even if you are not focusing on candle flame scrying, begin your wax scrying by gazing into the flame of the candle for a minute or two in total silence. This will help you make the transition from the fast everyday world to the logical left brain way of thinking.

The Traditions of Wax Scrying

Beeswax has been used in candles since medieval times, but, because it was expensive, people would usually have only one or two precious beeswax candles for scrying. Tallow or animal fat candles were created by the Romans or some claim in ancient Egypt and were also used. Because they were so smoky, candle smoke divination was an important part of the scrying.

Traditionally, candle scrying was practiced on Halloween, once called Samhain or Summer's End. The festival lasted for three days from dusk on October 31st. In Christian times, these days are called All Hallows Eve, All Saints or All Hallows Day on November 1st, and All Souls Day on November 2nd.

Another domestic candle festival was Candlemas Eve on February 1st. In pre-Christian times this was the festival of light for the Celtic Goddess Brighid. Her myths became incorporated with the Irish St. Bridget in the Christian tradition, whose special day was February 1st.

On Candlemas Eve, candles were put in the windows and green rushes scattered in the hall with the words "Holy Bridget you are welcome in our home and our hearts. Come in out of the cold, will you, and get warm by the fire?"

Candlemas, which is held on February 2nd, remained a major festival of candles right through Victorian times. People would make candles on the evening before to last for the coming months. On the actual day, church and household candles were blessed in a special service. Every parishioner was given a blessed beeswax candle believed to keep fire, storm, and danger away from the house. It also seems that this was unofficially used for candle and wax divination concerning important family matters.

In non-Celtic lands, wax divination has been transferred to New Year's Eve, and young women would look for the initials of their true love, known or unknown, forming in wax on the surface of the water. In total darkness, except for the candles in the water beneath the initials, at the last stroke of midnight the image of the desired lover would be seen. In the country, molten lead was cast into a metal bucket of cold water to create the initials (very spectacular but dangerous).

The Magic of Wax Scrying

Wax scrying, similar to candle scrying, is considered magical because the candle is a representation of the four basic elements—Earth, Air, Fire, and Water—once thought to be contained in every life form.

The body or form of the candle represents the Earth, the smoke the Air, the flame the Fire, and the melting wax the Water.

The Four Elements are combined and transformed as the candle is lit and the wax melts and hardens, creating the fifth magical Element: Aether, Spirit, or Akasha.

This magical Element, formed as the wax from the candle makes a new shape, seems to make the scryer very prophetic and clairvoyant.

In addition, wax images formed by dripping candle wax on water, which then hardened into a shape, are prized as lucky charms. Once cooled, they can be wrapped in a small piece of cloth tied with three knots, the number of magical completion. They are kept to bring protection, prosperity, and health, according to the image formed, until the wax naturally crumbles.

Interpreting Wax Images

There are two forms of wax scrying, the first burning a candle to perceive images in the melting and melted wax. These images can be seen running down the sides of the candle and around the holder or, if melted, on a flat metal holder, around the base. You can follow the path of past, present, and future by using three candles at the same time for each life stage. Or you can light a single candle for the three stages, blowing it out when partly melted, then relighting the partly melted candle twice, so the layers build up. This is very potent for seeing the influence of the past on the present and the present on the future.

The second form of wax scrying involves creating images on the surface of water by dripping one or more colored candles onto a bowl of water. This second method gives clear images, both in the molten moving wax and then the hardened wax image floating on the surface.

You can use wax scrying for decision-making using either method by asking a specific question and interpreting the image made by the fallen wax. This allows a message to come from your own higher wisdom, an angel, or a Spirit Guide.

You can also use wax scrying to channel messages from wise ancestors, angels, and guides, and nature essences or past worlds or lives by either method.

Finally, wax on water can create a doorway to other dimensions in the water, such as the past and past lives, or into Astral realms such those inhabited by power animals, nature spirits, angels, and Spirit Guides.

Choosing Your Candles for Wax Scrying

A good-quality wax candle where the color goes all the way through is essential. Some cheaper candles are dipped, and if you scratch the surface you will see the white within. These are not satisfactory for our purposes, unless you use darkened water as the candle wax appears white on the surface. You can ask in a store or by e-mail if the color goes all the way through. Some modern practitioners prefer using vegetable wax candles, such as palm or soy, instead of paraffin for environmental reasons. Tea lights, the kind of tiny candle in a foil base, disappear as they burn; these are useless for wax scrying.

White is fine for ordinary wax scrying as long as they are good-quality, pure wax, but not effective for dripping on water unless you darken the water with ink or, more traditionally, with a mugwort infusion.

Beeswax is ideal either in its creamy undyed state or dyed with natural colorings. It has the advantage of being fast-burning for scrying in a hurry if you want to combine both kinds of wax scrying, and it has a wonderful fragrance as it burns. It also makes a series of small, distinct images if you use a colored beeswax or plain beeswax on darkened water. You can make larger single talismanic beeswax images on water, but these are not as easy as ordinary wax, as beeswax is much more solid. The separate images are very clear, but they tend not to swirl and merge together as with ordinary colored wax.

However, beeswax candles bring a very sacred quality to any scrying, for bees are associated with Mother Goddesses back from the early Neolithic Bee Goddess, whose image was found painted on a vase some time between 6400–6200 B.C. in Otzaki in Thessaly.

In medieval Christian times the Virgin Mary and her mother, St. Anne, who was patroness of bees and beekeepers, were also linked with beeswax candles. Traditionally, bees have been regarded as messengers between the Earth and heavens, and so beeswax scrying offers a natural link with your angels and spirit guides.

Church candles, the white pillar kind, will work for scrying unless made of pure wax, those tend to collapse inwards and disappear.

Because candles can be mislabeled or not labeled at all, buy one of each type initially and experiment. Then when you have the right candles for wax scrying you can order a lot in different colors. The same is true of Internet orders—price alone is not a guide.

Best of all for candle wax scrying are long, slender candles that will create fascinating shapes as they melt around the candlestick, similar to wax sculptures.

You can also use a squat candle on a flat metal tray with a spike and carefully tip the molten wax on to the tray (make sure it is really wide enough not to spill over the edges) to create a series of images, which is good if you are in a hurry.

Colors

Stronger colors tend to be better for all forms of wax scrying, and you may find a particular candle color works well for you.

However, colors do have specific meanings and you can choose candle colors related with the matters about which you are asking or use the zodiacal color with the glyph scratched in the side. These are on pages 82–83 in Chapter 4. I have also listed their incenses or oils you can burn for the different candles.

In practical terms dark blue or purple on water gives very clear images if you are new to the art.

Asking Questions With Wax on Water

Dropping candle wax onto water is one of the easiest and most effective ways of receiving answers to questions or channeling messages from Spirit Guides, ancestors, angels, or even a departed relative. If you have not practiced wax scrying before, begin with this method. Once your eye is tuned into wax images, you will be able to work with just a candle.

You will need a light-colored ceramic or glass bowl the size of a cereal or dessert bowl for individual images and to create a single large talisman. A larger bowl is best for making several images for a group of people. Glass cookware bowls of the relevant size are ideal for wax water scrying. Experiment until you get the right bowl of the right size for your wax water scrying and keep it just for that. It should be heat-resistant, though the water will absorb a lot of the heat.

For a group, the best option is a cast iron pot similar to a witch's cauldron, even if you are not involved in Wicca at all. You can pick these up from New Age outlets or garage sales of old houses, but check that the one you buy is iron and heat-proof.

The first time you use your bowl, sprinkle it with sea salt, add bubbling tap water, and swirl it three times clockwise, three times counterclockwise, and three times clockwise again to purify it, then pour the water out under running water. After use, you can rinse it well with water, dry it with a special cloth you keep, and store it with your scrying tools.

You will also need a long, thin pure wax candle in either deep blue or purple, or the color appropriate to your question. Set it behind the bowl. If you wish, you can light two different-colored candles in different holders, one on either side of the bowl, and hold one in each hand for scrying. With practice, you can use four different colors, set in holders, two on either side of the bowl. Half-fill the bowl with water.

Next, light the candle(s). If you are using more than one scrying candle, light them from left to right and then the incense from the right-hand scrying candle in silence. Look into the flame of the scrying candle or each of the candles left to right and still your mind for a minute or two, even if you are not using candle flame scrying.

Then ask for protection and wisdom from your Spirit Guide, your Guardian Angel or one of the Archangels, an ancestor, or the God/Goddess using one of the methods I suggest for protection or ask for protection. Ask also that you see only what is of beauty and of worth.

If you wish you can say, "I am (add your first name) and I seek...." You can specify what you would like to be shown—for example an image or images to answer your question, or to receive a sign or message in the wax from your Guardian Angel, a spirit guide, an ancestor, or a past world. In this case instead of saying, "I am," say, "I seek wisdom from (name focal presence) if it is right to be at this time."

Far more exciting is to leave it entirely open and ask that you will see what is right for you in the wax.

Receiving Wisdom

Transfer your gaze slowly from the candle flame to the surface of the water and back again several times without seeking any particular pictures to build up the connection between the fire and water.

If you are using one candle, pick it up in the hand you write with and, very slowly, drip the wax drop by drop on to the surface of the water, in a gentle circular movement from the center outwards so it swirls and takes form. It may make a number of images or just one, and it will usually swirl together, harden, and make a single shape. With beeswax, you can add layers on top to merge.

A spoken answer to your question will come into your mind or, alternatively, a message from your angel or Guardian.

If using more than one candle, work much faster and swirl them on the surface so the colors combine before the first one hardens.

You can alternatively use wax on water to answer specific questions for someone else. He or she can drip the wax on a larger bowl of water set between you, and you can both interpret its significance to the question, or you can both use a candle each at the same time.

Whether for yourself or someone else, let the wax harden. When it is formed and floating, lift the shape from the water carefully and put it on a wooden or ceramic surface to dry. It will have formed a distinct shape. I have seen people create dragons, goddesses, angels, animals, birds, or sometimes a key, a doorway, or a heart. The shape may be of an angel if you asked to connect with an angel, but this may not always be so.

Carefully wrap the wax charm in cloth or waxed paper when it is dry and you can focus on it before sleep or when beginning past life scrying. When it crumbles, you need a new symbol.

After the scrying, write down or draw the moving images you saw and allow connections to occur spontaneously in your mind between them to answer your question or form a coherent message. Then in your scrying journal write up the experience and how any wax talisman formed represents the power or protection you most need, which may be entirely different from expected.

Future Readings

At a personal change point such as a birthday, or a recognized festival such as Halloween or New Year's Day, use a really big bowl and one candle.

You need a tape recorder so you can describe your images as they appear. For example, *January* (drop the wax), *a fat happy frog leaping in the air* (a good sign for the beginning of fertility and prosperity moving into your life), *February* (drop more wax, swirl water), *the frog is changing into a boat on a calm seas* (maybe a trip overseas or maybe you and your partner will decide to try for a baby while on vacation), *March* (drop wax, swirl water), and so on through the 12 months until you have an image for each of the months.

Afterward, you can draw the 12 images and allow your psychic senses to add information, explaining how they fit into your known plans. Keep your predictions and see how they shape up during the months ahead.

Wax and Water Group Scrying

This method is popular at parties and festivals such as Halloween or New Year's Eve, as a quiet family activity after supper, or with a group of close friends to help make a family decision or to help one of you work out a problem.

Start out by getting a large, glass bowl or cauldron of clear water. At the back of it, set a horseshoe of four candles in strong colors (for example, bright red, blue, orange, and green). Again, buy the kind where the color penetrates right through the candle for best effect. Choose four people to light the candles, from left to right as you face them.

As each person lights the candle he or she should name aloud the main question that concerns everyone or the question and the name of the person you are working for. This way it is said four times to build up the power. You can ask questions for different people one after the other by rinsing out the bowl between questions.

Each of you should gather around the front and sides of the bowl. Focus on the candlelit water for a minute or two without trying to discern any images. Allow your minds to go blank and merge your consciousness with the water.

Then each of the four chosen people (two candles each if there are only two of you) should take a candle in the power hand, the one you write with (unless the other hand feels more natural), and at a prearranged signal start to make patterns on the water with the colors. Everyone should call out and point to images as the molten symbols appear until the wax is hard and the bowl quite full.

Now study the hardened image(s) in the water. Each of you should give as much information about each image in turn, such as what you see, hear, and feel.

If it is a love issue, you may get wax initials; if the person asking looks beneath the initials, he or she may see an image of the right lover.

You can also limit yourself to three candles and make separate images in turn, the first image for the past, the second the present, and the third the future. With a huge bowl, you can let everyone have a different candle color. Set the candles on a separate table and stand around the bowl, adding wax at the same time to make a picture or series of related images.

When the wax images are set, you can either wrap each separately in greaseproof paper or bubble wrap and keep them in a drawstring bag as a family good luck charm. Give them to the person for whom they were made to answer the question.

Floating Candles

Another very effective method of wax on water imitates the natural movement of wind on water. This is done with floating candles.

Take three or four floating candles in the colors that relate to the area of your life or situation about which you are concerned. You can, if you wish, use fragrant ones and allow the scent to heighten your intuitions. Half-fill a clear glass bowl with water. Add clear glass nuggets or small quartz crystals to the bottom of the bowl so that the light will reflect on them. As you do so, make a wish or statement of power as you gently drop each crystal into the water. If your concern is money, you can drop a coin in the bowl as well. You can either ask a specific question, or focus on an issue that is of importance or a decision you have to make.

Place the candles in a circle on the water and light them in a clockwise formation. Extinguish all other lights and leave a window open so that there is a slight breeze. If the candles are not moving, turn the bowl nine times clockwise.

Half-close your eyes and allow pictures to develop in your mind, stimulated by the patterns on the water. Do not force symbols, but do not dismiss any as improbable or try to rationalize or analyze them. The process is entirely spontaneous. As the pattern of light changes, you may identify four or five consecutive images.

Afterward, write or draw any pictures and see what ideas form. If you find this process difficult, try telling yourself a story about the images. You will find answers to your original question and perhaps others you had not realized you needed to ask.

Also try floating candles on black-colored water with inks, a mugwort infusion, or strained, cold black tea or coffee.

Wax Candle Scrying

This can be used either as part of candle scrying or as a preliminary to the wax in water—or be a scrying art in its own right. If you are artistic, creative, or imaginative you will find it easy almost at once, but we can all learn the technique.

After dark, unless using the candle for wax on water (in which case choose a darker part of the room), light a single, slender candle in a tall candlestick and center yourself by gazing into the flame. Add a pinch of salt and ask that you be shown what it is you need to know. You can ask that you will only see and hear what is of worth and that the wisdom comes with light and love from whatever source of goodness.

This can be used for answering questions, but your wax sculptures are most potent in offering insights into your life. They are very good for triggering clairaudient messages from angels, Guides, or the recently deceased, who may send a symbol in the wax with a personal meaning as well as a message in your mind. Keep it all open ended as to who will speak.

Unless you are lighting beeswax (which begins to overflow almost at once), choose a relatively fast-burning wax candle (you can buy very small, high-quality ones in New Age stores, or look at labels for burning times). This is a good form of divination to carry out while using Tarot cards, runes, a mirror, or a crystal ball while the wax melts. You could also use the time to work on your symbol system or when you want to meditate, using the scrying candle flame as a focus.

If possible, use this quiet time and the slow, sinuous movement of the melting wax to connect with an older, slower time frame. Even divination can become instant, and the mental discipline of watching a slowly changing wax formation helps to slow us down.

If you are not looking at the candle at all times because you are writing, tune in by centering back with the flame every two or three minutes and let the flowing wax suggest its evolving images to you. These will change more rapidly as the candle burns lower. Do not burn the candle right through, as you get better shapes if about a third of the candle is still left. You can relight it on another occasion to see how the matter under question has developed since the last reading.

Look through half-closed eyes at the melting wax, and imagine that an artist is painting an ever-changing scene so the colors become shapes, blur and merge, and then take a new, richer form.

Draw the evolving images in your scrying journal, following the contours of the candle wax at different stages with your pen. You may perceive entirely new visions and insights when you look back at the drawings.

What is the slow, flowing build-up of wax saying to you, and what messages does it suggest in your mind? Look at the wax around the candle holder as well as the shapes forming on the sides of the candle.

When about a third is left, blow out the flame if it has not gone out and look first at the more external signs for general information.

Reading the External Signs in the Wax

Patterns in the Wax

These should be read when the wax is cool:

- Wax forming to the left of the candle indicates a "no" or "wait" response to your question.
- Wax to the right indicates that the time is right to act, or to ask as the response will be favorable.
- Wax evenly distributed says that you should seek the help of others.
- Wax gathered and set around the top of the candlestick advises going it alone.
- Thin strands of wax such as icicles down the sides of the candlestick and candle itself suggest that success will come through a series of steps—not always easy, but exciting.

ℜ   Waves of wax down the side are a sign of love and fidelity.

ℜ   A pool of wax accumulated around the base if marked or indented talks about success with money.

ℜ   A smooth pool around the base can indicate that efforts may not pay off or that others are draining your energy and resources.

ℜ   Jagged peaks and horizontal or diagonal points can herald restlessness and the need to travel or move on.

ℜ   Circles or spirals in the cooled wax are a sign of fertility and creativity.

ℜ   Deep grooves can be indicative of resistance to change by others or petty quarrels that you should step back from or they will wear your down.

ℜ   Squares indicate the need for security and stability, and satisfactory home and property.

ℜ   Triangles are for spiritual powers, for fertility, for good luck, and for all matters of increase.

ℜ   Flower shapes talk of health, healing, and new love and trust.

ℜ   Tiny dots represent small amounts of money or alternatively, a very busy time socially.

ℜ   Angels signify blessings coming.

ℜ   Stars indicate fame or incredibly good luck.

Reading the Inner Visions

Now look at your fabulous wax sculpture. Similar to modern art, it is open to your interpretation and you may see a whole scene, a collection of figures or animals, a boat on a sea, forests and waterfalls, or tall castles and palaces.

Find a single physically etched doorway or gate formed out of lines and shapes into the scene. Be creative and imaginative so you can see the images in their context, the wax people in a house, a temple or marketplace, the dragon guarding her store of gems underground or rising high in the sky. Then ask what this developing scene says to you either about your present life or future, or what messages are coming from your Guardians.

Look back at the drawings you made of the partially melted candle and notice how this final form is the end of a series of stages or facets that together will offer guidance.

Past, Present, and Future

You can work with three separate candles: purple for the past, blue for the present, and white for the future in a row left to right.

Total darkness is best. Light the candle of the past, then from it the candle of the present, and the candle of the future from the candle of the present.

First, put salt in the flame of the candle of the past. Ask that you may learn from the past what is most helpful to you in the present and what you could/should leave behind. Put a pinch of dried sage or rosemary into the flame of the candle of the present, asking that you may see what is of worth to take forward to the future and what must be healed before moving on. Finally, in the flame of the candle of the future, add a pinch of dried thyme or basil, asking to see the future path ahead that best could be travelled.

Focus on each of the candle flames in turn, making three columns in your scrying journal: one for the past, one for the present, and one for the future. Use the three lights to write by.

Scry in each candle flame in turn as on pages 83–85 in Chapter 4 and let an image appear in or around the flame and the in flame reflected in the melting wax around the wick. Record any images and words that come into your mind, or impressions in the appropriate column, even as mini-sketches if you wish. Then meditate on the flame of the past until the wax begins to melt. Again note any images in the moving wax

Do the same with the present and then with the future, moving from one to the other, but always centering in each flame first. This time wait until the candles are about a third burned down and blow out first the candle of the past, saying, "I leave in the past what belongs to the past and take forward what I have learned or gained."

Blow out the candle of the present, saying, "I take from the present what brings hope and has firm foundations and I heal whatever hurts or is unworthy."

Finally, blow out the candle of the future, saying, "The time is not yet here, but I take the guidance as to the paths of beauty and happiness that I may follow in due time."

As before, study your three sculptures and make notes to be combined with your other insights to see, and, most importantly, to determine the paths ahead.

You can alternatively use the same candle for all three stages. On the first night burn a third of the candle for the past, the second third on the next night, and let the candle burn through on the final night for your future journey. This way, over the three days, new layers of wax will build up and transform the old formation.

Chapter 8

Ink and Oil Scrying

Though water was an early means of divination, by 4000 B.C.E. in ancient Babylonia, scryers were adding oils and ink to the surface of the water to create tangible moving images. Natural divination was moving within the realms of the priesthood and professional scryers, which meant more complex rules and interpretation.

Ink Scrying

But oil scrying still continued within the province of house and home, especially in ancient Egypt, Greece, and Rome, to which it travelled from the Middle East. It was popular because these were hot lands where pure oil was plentiful and the main form of lighting was the oil lamp.

Ink scrying also originated in the Middle East when people began to keep written records. The medieval European magicians inherited these old arts from books brought back from the Holy Land after the Crusades from the 12th century onward. The books themselves were Arabic copies or Latin or Greek originals of plundered classical documents—many of which reflected the magick of ancient Egypt.

The ancient Egyptian Thoth, god of wisdom, writing and magick, and Hecate, the ancient Greek and Roman Crone or Grandmother Goddess of the triple crossroads where past, present, and future meet, are two deities associated with ink scrying. I am choosing Metatron as the focus of dedication. He was a favorite source of wisdom for medieval magicians and seems appropriate as the patron of modern Westernized ink scrying.

Metatron

The Archangel Metatron is called the Angel of the Lord, and in the Kabbalah he is placed at the top of the Tree of Life, as the closest Archangel to God's throne.

Metatron was the prophet Enoch. After death, Enoch's body was transformed into flame and he became surrounded by storms, whirlwinds, thunder, and lightning (fire is one of the attributes of the Archangel).

Because Enoch was a scribe or recorder during his lifetime, Metatron became the heavenly scribe. He lived in the Seventh Heaven, recording all heavenly and earthly events in what are often known as the Akashic Records.

Metatron is the tallest of the Archangels and is described as a huge pillar of brilliant white light, with 36 pairs of wings, a scroll whose contents are hidden from sight, and a pen.

His candle color is maroon red or white, and his fragrances are carnation, cedar, juniper, and lemongrass.

Ink Scrying

Ink scrying has remained popular in the Middle East to the present day. It is also still practiced as in earlier times by Hindu wise men. One early Middle Eastern version involved tipping ink into the palm of the hand and reading the formations created by the lines and grooves. However, that is a very messy method and you may find the floating method more acceptable.

Ink scrying can answer any question, including specific issues or choices concerning partners, love, family, and your immediate circle at work. You can also inquire about any study or learning, creative, artistic, or literary ventures; life change points; and decisions about home moves, especially involving relocation, downsizing, or bringing change to a lifestyle.

Ink scrying is traditionally carried out in the hour before sunset when the light is soft but still clear, and the daily noise and activity is slowing. It helps to have natural light on the water, but not directly reflected sunlight shining into it.

It can also be practiced by more than one person, each having a different colored ink and brush, and adding a drop at a time to the water until an image is formed. The image is then interpreted jointly. For this reason you can make joint family decisions with ink scrying or help a friend or client who may be nervous about more formal divinatory methods such as tarot.

Use a white, shining metal or clear glass bowl as large as you wish. Keep this bowl separate for ink scrying so you can dedicate it for this purpose

Red, blue, purple, green, and black inks give the clearest images. You can use more than one color, adding them one at a time with different brushes. However, this must be done rapidly before the entire water colors and obscures the images. You can get a lovely effect as one color starts to sink and spread as another falls on the surface.

You can buy special magical inks with exotic names such as Pigeons' Blood, though, of course, this is made from plant pigment and various exotic herbs. Magical inks are very expensive, but they make beautiful flowing images. However, you can just as easily use ordinary waterproof writing ink, dripped on to the surface of the water with a very fine lined brush or a pen with a nib. You can buy these kinds of pens and brushes from an art or specialist stationery store. Some practitioners use an eye dropper, but I prefer a very slender good quality bristle brush. If you are using more than one color, have a separate brush or pen for each color. Put the open inks around the bowl. You can then cleanse and empower them along with the bowl.

If you want to be totally 21st century, for ink scrying in a hurry, use a plastic ink-filled cartridge, the sort you fit inside cartridge pens, but do not insert it inside a pen. Instead, pierce the end and squeeze it drop by drop on to the surface of the water. You are not being sacrilegious to the old ways. The old-fashioned kinds of pen and inks we associate with ink scrying were used in earlier times by officials for mundane tasks such as record- or account-keeping, as well as for magic.

Dedicating the Bowl, Pens, and Inks

Dedicate your equipment the first time you intend to ink scry and then rededicate the bowl, pens, and inks every time you add or replace a tool. Cleansing and empowerment is normally all you need to do before the scrying begins.

When not in use, keep your inks and pens in a special pouch or case, and the bowl in a natural fabric cloth or bag. Dark blue and purple are good colors for the fabric. Set a blue or purple cloth underneath the scrying bowl; replace it when it becomes stained.

Make a circle of your red, black, purple, green, and blue inks and alternate them with your pens or brushes. Put the empty bowl in the center. Then light a white or maroon candle in the center to the left of the bowl and from it light in turn four incense sticks in any of Metatron's fragrances or the more ceremonial dragon's blood, frankincense, or sandalwood. Set the four incense sticks in holders or small jars around the outside of the circle of inks and pens, evenly spaced at 12, 3, 6, and 9 o'clock positions on an imaginary clock face. Use the same fragrance for all four incenses and sit facing the 12 o'clock positioned incense, which is equal to North.

Have a jug of clear water outside the circle where you can easily reach it. Fill up the bowl halfway, then take the 12 o'clock incense and write over the bowl using the incense stick as a pen. "I am (add your name in the smoke)." You can speak the words aloud if you wish at the same time. Be careful not to drop ash in the water. If necessary, smoke-write slightly to the side of the bowl, but still in the air.

Return the incense to its holder and, taking the 3 o'clock (East) incense, write over the bowl, speaking if you wish aloud, "Metatron, bless these tools." Return it to the holder and take the 6 o'clock (South) incense, writing in smoke and if you wish speaking aloud, "Metatron bring me wise visions." Finally, take the 9 o'clock position (West) incense and draw a complete smoke circle clockwise just above the surface of the table to enclose the outside of the tools and the incense sticks, but not the jug. Say aloud or in your mind, "Metatron protect this endeavor." Return that incense to its place. Leave the incenses to burn through. You can now practice ink scrying in the bowl. (See the following section for details.)

After scrying, blow out the candle, saying the name of Metatron three times aloud or in your mind. Add more water from the jug to the ink-stained water, swirl it, and empty the bowl under a running tap, rinsing the bowl and leaving it to dry before putting away.

For a faster, less-formal ink cleansing and empowerment before a scrying session, set the inks, brushes, and empty bowl as before, then light the candle and the four incense sticks. Half-fill bowl with water. Using only the first incense stick (the one positioned at 12 o'clock) draw smoke spirals over the bowl and tools, both counterclockwise and clockwise for cleansing and empowering. As you do so, say aloud or in your mind, "Be filled with light in the name of Metatron." Cleanse as I previously suggested after the scrying.

You can work outdoors, putting your candle in a heat-proof open glass container so the wind does not blow it out.

Beginning Ink Scrying

After dedicating your tools and bowl for the first time, practice dripping a single colored ink by your chosen method on to the surface of the water. If you use too much, you will color the water almost at once.

Experiment until you know the amount needed to create a clear, initial surface image. This gradually changes as the ink moves lower. You may get another image on the bottom and, if you are lucky, intermediate images as it swirls through the water. You may find that moving the bowl slightly helps the ink to form patterns and shapes. Try adding more ink and then a second color. The only way to get the right amounts is to experiment.

When you have mastered the technique and can create and identify images, ask a question or concentrate on an issue as you drop in the ink, using more than one color if you wish. As the ink swirls and sinks, you will find that the changing images explain or add knowledge about the first image. You may see a whole picture rather than a single image. If the water is not yet colored, add more ink to make a second image.

If you do want to add more images because you need more information, once the water becomes dark-colored, pour out the water, wash out the bowl, and refill it with fresh water. The new images will continue naturally where you left off. Note any feelings the images evoke and any words that come into your mind as well as any natural associations.

If you begin scrying using the last light of the day, you can, once the water is colored dark with the ink, light candles around the black or dark blue water and gaze into that for further clarification. Hold the bowl of darkened water between your hands and tip it gently. About halfway down, the image or images will often appear white against the blue or black as the color parts for a moment.

Structuring Your Reading

I enjoy the open-ended approach that was previously described. However, there are times when it will be more useful to structure the reading by designating in advance the number of images you will study. Four with an optional fifth works well for ink scrying, and you can assign meanings that feel right for each image before the individual reading.

The same image from the original ink dropped may spontaneously change into the other images, but it is up to you to add extra ink at any time for clarification. This is a matter for you to decide as the reading progresses. If the water colors too early, wash the bowl out and refill it.

- **Image 1: The Root of the Matter.** What the real underlying issue is and the factors that may not be clear to the conscious logical mind at the start of the reading.

- **Image 2: The Head of the Matter.** What is expected to happen if you stay on your present course and people act the way they currently do; the predictable future.

- **Image 3: The Heart of the Matter.** What you really feel and what you really want.

- **Image 4: The Spirit of the Matter.** This is often the image created as the ink shape sinks, changes, and maybe rests on the bottom, telling you what is totally unexpected, both in terms of help and obstacles.

Oil Scrying

Oil scrying was practiced in ancient Egypt, Greece, and Rome, and Middle Eastern lands as far back as prehistoric times when the first open shell oil lamps were used.

There are two methods for oil scrying: The first one involved hot oil in lighted oil lamps, and the second involved studying cold oil stored in vats or dropping cold oil on the surface of water. Oil on water remained a popular method among ordinary ancient Egyptians and you can occasionally still see this demonstrated in tourist bazaars on stalls where highly colored scented oils are for sale.

Another ancient Middle Eastern method involved covering the inside of a white cup with sesame oil or a similar thick, dark oil and using the cup as a concave mirror. I have witnessed a similar technique in a home I visited in Cairo where thick Turkish coffee left clinging to the inside of a cup was read, using the white markings of the cup that appeared through the coffee to create the pictures. In both cases, a half-circle of candles were directed to reflect light into the cup as it was held in the hands of the scryer.

Oil scrying of any kind is very good for showing the road ahead if this is unclear; untangling dilemmas; seeing the way through conflicts and around obstacles; for revealing unexpected opportunities and ways of bringing light into a situation or relationship that seems hopeless; and for exploring the past and other dimensions (see the following Eye of Horus technique).

Oil scrying, similar to ink, is traditionally practiced in the hour before sunset, outdoors if possible, or otherwise where you would be able to see the beginnings of sunset as you work. Hot oil scrying is linked to sunrise and is said to work best for personal individual readings. However, you can carry out oil divination any time you need to, as long as there sufficient clear, soft, and natural light. Soft light reflections on the water can be helpful, but not bright sunlight. It is best if you can catch the red and pink sunset or sunrise rays in the water. Always remain silent while oil scrying.

If you are working during sunset, sit with your back to the West or the direction of sunset so the colors fall on the surface of the water. The actual direction of sunset differs slightly during the year. Sunset is only directly due West on the Equinoxes, around March 21st and September 21st–22nd. The same is true of the Eastern sunrise.

For an alternative, as the shadows deepen, light a pure white or beeswax candle at the back of the bowl to cast light on the oil and water. I prefer more natural light, but this is a matter of choice.

Dedicating Your Oil Lamp or Oil Scrying Dish

Whether you practice hot or cold oil scrying, you will need to dedicate whatever tools you are using to scry. At the same time, you can bless the oil you intend to use and any other oil scrying equipment. Pour your chosen oil into a smaller decorative bottle if you prefer. Try to keep the oil specially for any scrying. Because the dedication is so simple, you can use it for cleansing and empowering, and then closing down any session.

Thoth, the ancient Egyptian scribe, was the father of the deities and present at creation. He translated thought into word and animated the sun. He was also God of law, writing and spoken word, medicine, healing, and mathematics, and had command over magical knowledge. It was believed that Thoth would be present during oil scrying both as protector and to make the meaning of the images clear in the mind of the perceiver.

Depicted as an ibis or baboon with a crescent or full moon disk on his head, Thoth is also seen with his magical palate, recording the words and commands of the deities and writing the laws for humankind.

Thoth

Because Thoth's words were believed to contain the power that brought the sun into being, the dedication is very simple and spoken aloud—the only spoken words during the scrying.

Thoth

Set the items in a row left to right with small spaces in between them and touching each in turn. Over each, say over each, "By Thoth be cleansed, by Thoth be blessed, by Thoth protected and brought to life, that truth maybe be revealed and hope restored by the power of Thoth."

Then you can now set up your scrying materials and begin. After scrying, return all the items to their place and touch each in reverse order, repeating the same words, substituting the words "and set to rest" for the earlier "brought to life." Wash out the bowl or clean the lamp and leave to dry naturally.

Cold Oil Scrying

I have started with cold oil scrying because it is easier to set up and to see images with the physical eye. Many oil scryers never use anything except cold oil scrying because of safety considerations and because it is the clearest oil medium. Read through the hot oil scrying section to see which one suits you best.

Because oil constantly moves, when dropped on to cold water, it is a very effective method for allowing psychic images to unfold via the physical eye, simply by relaxing and watching the symbols emerge spontaneously from the Well of Wisdom as the oil floats, forms, and reforms. Be open to however and whatever way the insights come rather than worrying about seeing a set number of images or assigning them specific functions.

Until you are confident about perceiving images, use dark-colored oil that contrasts with the water in a clear glass or pale ceramic bowl. The cheaper, brightly colored room fragrance oils you buy for oil burners are ideal for cold oil scrying. Very dark virgin olive oil is traditional and gives stronger physical images than pale oil. You can also scry with pure essential oils, but choose ones that are yellow or brown.

As you become more experienced, work with paler oils such as olive, sunflower, almond, or the traditional clear palm oil (sometimes called oasis oil).

Cold Oil Scrying in Practice

Drip the oil drop by drop either through an eyedropper or using an old fragrance or essential oil bottle with a built-in dropper, or carefully drip it through the narrow neck of a very small bottle. (Ornate Egyptian glass perfume bottles are ideal and widely available in gift stores.) Use small amounts, be sparing with the oil, and pause between drops; experiment to get the right amount.

Allow the oil to swirl and form images on the surface in its own time and way, using only very gentle movements to turn the bowl and make fresh images with the existing floating oil. However, the new images often form from the old quite spontaneously. Relax your eyes and flow with the experience.

Once you are an expert in creating oil images, ask in your mind that Thoth will reveal to you what you need to know, or focus on an issue that is of importance, but maintain silence throughout.

Afterward, draw the random images you saw onto paper with a black pen and make connections expressed as lines that feel right to draw. Joining the images with a pen may bring options or associations you had not thought of. Oil scrying answers will develop further in the hours following the scrying so try to spend a quiet evening by candlelight with as little external sound as necessary.

Gateway Readings With Cold Oil

Eye of Horus

It was said in ancient Egypt that a single drop of oil on water might, if a scryer was blessed form the Eye of Horus, see visions of the far future. It is still considered lucky to see either the Eye of Horus on the surface of the water while oil scrying.

The Eye of Horus was a symbol of inspiration as well as protection in the Egyptian world. In fact there are two forms: one Horus eye faces left and the other to the right (shown above). The right eye is the Sun eye and white, and the other the Moon eye, sometimes colored black.

The Sun, or white eye, of Horus was linked with the eye of Ra, the Sun God, and with the magical mirror of Hathor. This would tell of the worldly or earthly fulfillment ahead. The Moon eye revealed hidden messages that the scryer needed to know.

Practitioners who carried the art into Europe identified a single perfectly round drop of oil on water as a magical mirror or doorway that gave visions of other realms and the long-term future of the seeker. You can create this doorway deliberately with practice. Sometimes, however, you will want to be open to naturally forming images or entrances.

To create this astral or spiritual window, mirror, or door-way of oil on the surface of the water, very carefully concentrate one or two drops of oil in the center of the bowl of water. Once formed, these take you into other dimensions. As you make the entrance, you can specify whether you wish to look through the doorway to see beyond present blockages or to meet a particular Guide or ancestor. (See also Chapter 7.)

Soften your eye focus by half-closing them. Softly breathe in and out and picture the doorway, window, mirror, or eye slowly opening and expanding to form a shimmering entrance of pure light that fills the bowl. You may physically *see* a single symbol in the entrance or one rapidly changing into another. Instead, there may be a face of your Guide, Guardian Angel, or beloved ancestor who may show you a symbol that has personal meaning for you. You may hear a message in a soft, melodious voice that may be familiar from other spiritual work if you already work with angels and Guides. You can also ask to glimpse into a past world that has meaning for you.

Only make one doorway per scrying session, and then wash out the bowl. You can ask on subsequent occasions to return to the same place or vision, and, often after scrying, the scenes or spiritual beings will appear in your dreams with further knowledge for you.

If the doorway does not appear, you know it is time to concentrate on more earthly concerns, so look for images as normal.

Hot Oil and Oil Scrying

The earliest oil lamps were made from large sea shells. Ancient Egyptians and ancient Babylonians originally used an oil lamp, a stone shaped as a low open dish with deep sides, and a strip of white linen coiled in the oil, with an end hanging over the end of the dish to act as the wick.

In this kind of open lamp, the movements of the hot oil were studied as well as the flame (very hazardous). Occasionally, there are replicas found of those used in more remote Roman Empire outposts, as well as from early Egypt and other parts of the Middle East.

In the enclosed kind of oil lamp that became popular in later ancient Egypt, Greece, and Rome, the flame was the focus of the scrying and around it were the visions. It was believed that the shadows on either side of the flame indicated the presence of the deities who brought the visions.

Enclosed oil lamps were hung outside homes in ancient Egypt and later in Greece and Rome on the evening before or on the actual Midwinter Solstice to protect the home from spirits and persuade the sun to shine again on the shortest and darkest day of the year. One would be kept indoors for scrying as the first light came the following morning, because the sun had been reborn.

With enclosed oil lamps, the kind you can most easily buy today, the flame itself is studied according to the rules of candle scrying (see Chapter 4.) But here I will focus on working with the hot oil in the older open lamp formation so that you can see the images within the bubbling oil. This is a very effective method of scrying as long as you are very careful. It is certainly not a method to use around pets or children. Remember: Never try to put out oil that is burning too fiercely with water. You must cut off the air supply with a metal lid.

A safer alternative is the modern electric-powered lava lamp, which can get very hot if touched but follows exactly the same principles as open lamps. You can occasionally obtain flat, open, Egyptian-style oil ceramic lamps with a floating wick and a heatproof lip (small handle used for holding) for carrying in museum shops, as well as by mail order on the Internet.

Though olive or palm oil was traditionally used, you may prefer a scented lamp oil to relax the senses. I like to work with darker colored oils. If you use unfragranced oil, burn frankincense, myrrh, or sandalwood incense to help you to move beyond the everyday world.

Work at sunset or in the early-morning light as the sun is rising for any heated oil scrying.

Using a Fragrance Oil Burner for Hot Oil Scrying

My own favorite substitute for the elusive open lamp is a fragrance oil burner with a small candle beneath. Use the kind made of metal or with a heatproof glass or white ceramic bowl above the candle or small night light flame.

Fill the bowl about a third of the way either with a domestic fragrance burning oil or 10 to 15 drops of your favorite essential oil. With essential oil add cold water before lighting to bring the liquid up to a third. Set this on a low table so you don't have to get too near the hot oil.

In the evening sit with the burner in the East so you face West, or for early-morning scrying, place the burner on the East side of the table and sit on the West side facing East, so the first light illuminates the oil. Light the burner and formulate an area of your life where you would welcome guidance. Chant in a soft voice several times: "Lamp light, lamp bright, show to me what is to be." At this point, you can ask Thoth to assist if you wish.

As the oil begins to heat and the surface of the oil gently moves, half-close your eyes and allow scenes to build up and flow one into the other to make a story on the surface. Until recently, I have worked by connecting a series of single images formed by the heating oil, but the story method in which you are the hero or heroine seems much more fruitful, especially for life path decisions.

For effect, top off the oil by adding cold fragrance oil or water to the essential oil in the burner bowl rather than the usual warmed water. You can also add a few drops of the cold essential oil if the fragrance is fading.

Sit far back, as this will cause the existing oil to bubble up suddenly, creating a vivid picture. Look into the smoke created by the heating oil and it will make patterns or shapes.

When you are ready, extinguish the flame. Close your eyes. In the fading fragrance, you will hear the words of the wise Thoth or a personal Guardian, slow and measured, telling you what you most need to know (even if you had not asked this at the beginning). Instantly, all the images and scenes will rush fast through your mind, one after the other, similar to a film, created by rearranging the out of sequence pictures you received in your scrying, into a coherent story abut you.

Best of all, the film in your mind will have an ending, and, if it is not what you desire, open your eyes and look into the now still oil and *see* what and how you can make that future different.

Chapter 9

Dream Scrying

Dreams are the perfect scrying medium if you are seeking answers to specific questions. This is done through a process called dream incubation. You can also connect with past worlds in deliberately induced dreams, or call on your Guardian Angel, Spirit Guides, or a deceased loved one.

As in any other form of scrying, you can use dreams to specify in advance what it is you wish to dream about. Of course, what you do see may be completely different from what you requested or expected, but it may answer the question in a far better way than you anticipated. What you see may also be what you really need to know before you can go on to deal with the issue contained in the question.

The History of Dream Scrying

Dream scrying is nothing new. Indeed, as early as 2000 B.C.E. in ancient Egypt, a dream book was written giving the meanings of dream images. It also included rituals to bring good dreams, how to discover what was unknown or being deliberately concealed by others, and, less positively, how to send bad dreams to enemies. We have a later copy of this information in the form of a papyrus, now in the British Museum, which was found in Thebes River in Upper Egypt. It dates back to 1350 B.C.E.

There were many famous ancient Greek and Roman dream temples where ordinary people went to carry out rituals and make offerings before sleeping within the temple precincts to experience prophetic dreams. Even magistrates would visit the temples before hearing difficult cases.

Dream healing was practiced by the ancient Greeks through a process derived from Egyptian dream practices. Most famous for healing dream incubation were the Aesculepian temples, which were sited at sacred wells and springs. Aesculapius was a Greek healer who lived during the 11th century B.C.E., and who after his death became god of healing.

The first shrine dedicated to Aesculapius was built in Athens in the fifth century B.C.E. by Sophocles. Other shrines followed in rapid succession, the most famous at Epidaurus. More than 300 active Aesculepian healing temples still existed throughout Greece and the Roman Empire in the second century C.E., visited by those seeking cures for all kinds of maladies.

Animal sacrifices were made and the dreamer would sleep on the skin of the sacrificed animal, which was usually a ram. Evening prayers or chants were held during the hour of the sacred lamps at twilight, and seekers would ask Aesculapius to bring them healing in their dreams.

When Aesculapius appeared to the dreamers in the dream state, he would tell them the medicine they should use and any treatment that should be followed. Sometimes his daughters Hygeia or Panacea, also associated with health and healing, would appear to dreamers. On certain occasions, the god would perform psychic surgery.

St. Madron's Well in Cornwall in southwest England may date back to similar times, though it was dedicated to the ancient Mother Goddess, later called Modron, by the Celts around the second century B.C.E.

The well has continued as a place of dream divination, both for love and healing, even today. When it was Christianized around the sixth century C.E., it was rededicated to an unknown saint.

The bed of St. Madron is a stone seat close to the well that was used for scryers to sleep on after having drunk the waters from the well and making an offering. Then, they would ask the goddess/saint to send them a vision of love or to bring them healing or fertility.

Cures were reported as late as the 17th century, when the local bishop reported that a severely crippled man, John Trelille, "received three admonitions in his dreams. He washed in St. Madron's Well and slept afterwards in St. Madron's bed, and was suddenly cured."

How Dream Clairvoyance Operates

The modern world is no different when it comes to using sleep time creatively to scry for answers that are revealed in dream scenarios and symbols. What is more, our own immune systems or powers of fertility are activated. Our psychic radar may, because of some unknown and unverifiable power within the dream, telepathically draw us in everyday life to a dream lover we saw in sleep when we asked about love. We know relatively little still about the hidden powers of the mind during sleep, and so, in this elusive form of scrying, we are still exploring exciting unknown territory

Sleep Scrying

Because we are in a relaxed state during sleep, our subconscious minds can take us beyond the limits of measured time, beyond the material planes of existence, and it seems far beyond the physical distances that could be traveled by a person during sleep.

Our clairvoyant powers are most active at night, whether you believe we are traveling in our minds, or that we use the spiritual body we all possess within our physical body to go walk about other dimensions during sleep.

Indigenous people from Siberia to sub-Saharan Africa call these nocturnal wanderings "astral" or "out of body sleep states." In them, they visit the wise ancestors they claim for wisdom and healing. In the modern world we can, in practice, create dreams to connect with angels, Spirit Guides, wise ancestors, or beloved family members who are no longer with us.

You need to prepare for sleep scrying just as much as you do any other kind of scrying. If you normally share a bed or bedroom, it is up to you whether you sleep with other people while dream scrying. Perhaps they would like to share the ritual. If your partner or roommate is nervous of the spiritual world or unsympathetic, pick a time when you can be totally alone. Dream scrying can be particularly potent if you have carried out another form of scrying during the day or evening, and will clarify what you saw, heard, and felt in the earlier ritual.

The following is a method that you can adapt for clairvoyant dream work to call whoever you wish to come to you in sleep, or to answer questions to which your conscious mind cannot find the answers.

The Water Dream Rite

Try, if possible, to avoid talking to anyone, whether by phone, by e-mail, or in person, in the hour before you make the connection. Instead, have a leisurely bath by candlelight. Use lavender or rose-scented candles, and lavender or rose essential oil or bath foam, as these are two fragrances most associated with sleep scrying as well as inducing a state of relaxation. Put on something loose and comfortable, and carry the candles to the bedroom.

Use rose, carnation, lavender, sandalwood, myrrh, or violent fragrance oil in a fragrance burner as these are effective for creating doorways into dreams. Incense is too heavy for the bedroom. Light additional small pink or lilac candles if you need to. Play soft music without words as background, especially if you live in a noisy area.

Now you need a scrying medium that will make the connection with the dreams world. Half-fill a smoked or dark glass with still mineral water. Move the candles so that candlelight shines on the water as you sit in bed holding the glass cupped between your hands. Look deep into the water for a minute or two until you are quite relaxed.

Ask softly aloud the question you need answered in your sleep, or speak the name of whoever you would like to see in your dreams: Guardian Angel, Spirit Guide, ancestor, or a departed beloved relation who gave you wise advice during their lifetime.

You can ask your chosen dream companion to answer a question or to give you advice that will best help in the days ahead. If you did earlier scrying with another method you can ask for clarification of what you learned. Instead, you could instead ask to see the past world that will best help you to find happiness in your present life

Alternatively, leave the dream scrying entirely open and say, "Come to me in my sleep and wake with me in my dreams you who will walk with me this night through the beautiful lands till morning."

Drink three drops from the glass and then blow out the light, saying, "When I drink again in the morning I will recall the wisdom of my dreams."

Set the glass by your bedside and as you drift into sleep, picture yourself looking deep into the water of the cosmic well of wisdom that holds all secrets, past, present, and future, and from all lands.

As soon as you wake in the morning, drink from the glass again and then look into the water. You will recall your dreams and any dream companions. Even if you end up not see, your chosen dream companion, as you look into the water you will be aware of dream symbols that, if you relax and keep staring into the glass, will reveal quite spontaneously the answers or information you need.

If you wake during the night, picture the deep well. In your mind look into it until you drift once more into sleep. Do not try to recall any dreams unless you wish to re-enter one at the point you woke; in which case re-create the last moments of the dream scene in your mind and walk back in your imagination.

You can also use this method to scry for an unknown lover by asking that he or she will reveal him- or herself to you in sleep (see later in the chapter and also Chapter 10 on using magical mirrors for love).

Crystal Dreams

Another powerful medium to induce psychic dreams is a crystal.

Use either an amethyst or rose quartz crystal sphere, or a small amethyst or rose quartz polished crystal, as these are the best for dream work. A selenite sphere, the white translucent moon crystal named after Selene, Roman goddess of the full moon, is another potent source of dream wisdom, especially if moonlight is shining through your bedroom window. The kind with a satin shimmering stripe around it is called Satin Spar and is a very powerful dream crystal.

Phantom quartz, clear and containing a ghost or outline of a crystal within, is another excellent dream crystal, particularly for past life dreams or for connecting with wise ancestors or recently deceased relations. Shimmering opal or angel aura is the crystal for angel or guide connections.

Follow the steps of the earlier ritual, but this time gaze within the crystal instead of the water and imagine a gateway and paths within it leading into the dream realms. Ask your question. Move the sphere or crystal so that the candlelight highlights the gateway of light within it. If you requested a dream companion, try to picture him or her waiting for you within the doorway.

When you extinguish the candles, put the crystal down close to your bed. Imagine in your mind the crystal expanding and enclosing you in its shimmering light. Walk towards the doorway and your waiting guardian, into sleep.

When you wake, look deep into the crystal (if necessary lighting a candle if it is still dark) and recall your dreams. Try to get up five or 10 minutes earlier than usual so you can sit quietly in the early-morning light or candlelight. Allow any forgotten aspects of your dreams to flow back naturally into your mind.

Ancient Egyptian Dream Scrying

To the ancient Egyptians, dreams were an important means of communication, both with the deities and with the ancestors. In sleep, both deities and deceased relations would respond favorably to petitions and offerings by giving unknown information about the daily world. They also interceded, it was believed, with higher cosmic powers and also warned and advised the living on future events.

To the Egyptians, the creative thought processes in sleep mirrored the process that creator god Ptah and Thoth, god of wisdom, used to bring the world into being. Indeed, Thoth was one of the deities believed to give counsel in dreams (see also oil scrying on pages 143–152). In the later Ptolemaic period, Serapis, regarded as the husband of the Mother Goddess Isis by the Romans, was the god of dreams. He was often depicted with a bull's head.

Methods of Obtaining Dreams and Night Visions

Now that you have worked with dream scrying you might like to explore the more complicated ancient Egyptian method of dream scrying.

Bes

The ancient Egyptians recognized that it was possible to create significant or psychic dreams to bring answers or solutions. One source of wisdom, especially on domestic matters, was Bes, the household dwarf god. He brought luck and protection to the household and all who were part of it, and so this fierce, rather ugly character was much loved and considered as a protective figure in sleep as well as to the waking.

Late in the evening before bed, would-be dreamers drew an image of Bes on their left hand, the hand that was believed to be linked to lunar and hidden knowledge.

They would then ask for Mother Isis's blessing upon a large, black dream cloth to amplify the secret dream knowledge, and they would wrap their left hand in the cloth.

The dreamers would not speak until bedtime, when they would enfold themselves in the dream cloth. The cloth was a form of sensory deprivation to shut out the external world.

Of course you don't even have to draw Bes. When using these old methods it is important to adapt them to what feels right for you; some people think Bes is spooky. I like him because he is a symbol of protection and is also a gatekeeper of dream wisdom with thousands of years of history behind him. You can find out more about him by searching his name on the Internet and maybe understand why I like and trust him so much.

Instead of Bes, you could draw the outline of an angel if you wanted to work with the wisdom of your Guardian Angel. You could also draw a heart for love, a flower for health and healing, a plane for travel, a house for property or relocation considerations, a pen if you wanted to publish a book, and so on.

Inducing a Significant Dream

About 10 minutes before bedtime, light frankincense or myrrh in the bedroom. If you have a small nightlight, that would be useful as well. On your left palm draw an outline of Bes with his crown of feathers in smudge-proof dark lipstick or eyebrow pencil, or use concentrated vegetable-based paint and a fine brush (test your skin for sensitivity). The original ink used contained some very strange ingredients not so suitable for modern dream scryers. If the idea of drawing an ancient Egyptian dwarf on your hand does not feel right, draw whoever or whatever feels right on your left palm.

Use conventional black ink to write on a small piece of white paper the question or request that will hopefully form the source of the dream.

Next, take a long, wide, dark scarf or shawl. You can ask Bes, Mother Isis, any favorite personal deity, your Guardian Angel, the God/Goddess, a Spirit Guide, or the powers of goodness and light to bless the garment and enfold you in protection during your sleep travels.

If you wish, say something such as "May the Guardian of truth come from his/her sacred place this night and visit me with dreams of truth and gentleness. May I see only goodness as I seek what is of worth and beauty with the highest intent."

Enfold yourself in the scarf and read the question aloud. Place it folded under your pillow. Blow out the light and lie in the darkness tracing the outline of Bes or your chosen symbol through the scarf and repeat the question as you drift into sleep.

Keep a pen and paper by the bed so whenever you wake you can write the symbols of your dream before it fades. Draw an image of Bes or your chosen symbol at the four corners before you begin recording your dreams. Say, "Bes (or your chosen protector), aid and make true my memory of this dream." Before you get up, look at the uncovered Bes or symbol on your hand and repeat the question for the final time. If you remain still and silent, the answer will come into your mind and you will see how the dream suggests the direction in which you should proceed. Wash your hand very carefully, thanking the guardians for their wisdom and protection.

Scrying for Love in Dreams

For hundreds of years or maybe longer, people have used dreams to discover the identity of a future lover, to connect with him or her in sleep, and hopefully to draw that lover telepathically into their lives in the days or weeks following the dream.

If you want to go for the more psychic theory, then an unknown lover we meet in a dream is a real person who may also dreaming at that moment, if not actively scrying for love in sleep. Because both people are on the dream plane at the same time and both need love, they may be drawn together mind to mind through telepathic signals in sleep. Sometimes only one person will recall the dream, usually the woman, though the man may have a sense of recognition at the first actual meeting.

If you are unattached in real life or unhappy in a relationship you may transmit "find me in the real world" signals that may be answered by someone who is also searching for new love. These vibes will be amplified if one of you is dream scrying for love.

Working on Carl Jung's theory that all coincidences are not chance, but meant to be, our inner radar may guide us to a particular place in the days after the dream at the same time the intended person (whom we saw in the dream) is also guided there apparently by accident.

A more psychological explanation is that we all have a number of potential future partners who could make us happy, though some people are convinced we all have just one who is totally right. Therefore, you may dream of a person whom your unconscious mind knows would make you happy, but not necessarily the choice your conscious mind would make. Because of the dream, you will be sending out very positive nonverbal attraction vibes to this potential nearly ideal lover when you do meet.

Chapter 10

Scrying With Mirrors

The magic mirror that reveals what is not yet known appears in fairytales and legends; remember Snow White? "Mirror, mirror on the wall, who is the fairest of us all?" asked the Wicked Queen.

When the magic mirror somewhat tactlessly informed the Queen that Snow White was the most beautiful of all, the Queen ordered Snow White's death.

The mirror later told the Queen that Snow White was hidden in the forest safe with the seven dwarves. It subsequently guided the wicked Queen to the place Snow White was hiding to deliver a poisoned apple.

When the Queen discovers she is still second in the beauty stakes and Snow White has been carried off by a handsome prince to live happily ever after, she shatters the mirror into a thousand pieces. Because the Queen has bound her fate with the mirror, she dies with it.

Of course the mirror was reflecting back the Queen's own fears about her fading looks and jealousy of Snow White. For deep down the Queen already knew that Snow White was the loveliest, and so in a sense she was answering her own question, as we often do with mirrors. The information is buried deep within us, beyond the range of the conscious mind. But the mirror will reveal the truth in images that are unmistakable, and, in the case of the Queen's s mirror, in rhyming verse.

The moral of the tale is not that magic mirrors are bad or dangerous, but that if we apply the insights and messages in the glass to our lives wisely, the magic mirror is our best friend and guide. However, if the scryer uses those same images to justify less-than-noble behavior, there is no point in blaming subsequent bad luck or negative results on fate.

The Mirror Revisited

Right from the first indication that Snow White was unbeatable in the glamour department, the wicked Queen could have accepted that maybe the adolescent Snow White was actually a pain in the butt to live with and made her own angst about ageing a million times worst.

The value of mirror scrying is to see ourselves as we really are and then decide what changes we want to make within ourselves or our lives. We should make the best of what we are and develop what we still could be in the most positive way.

Therefore, it is a very personal and, at times, painful art, as the Queen found, but it can open possibilities using the untapped potential we all possess whether 18 or 80.

The Mother of Mirror Scrying

Long before glass was made, polished metal was used for mirrors, especially copper and silver.

The invention of mirror scrying is attributed to the ancient Egyptians and, in particular, the goddess Hathor.

Hathor was the ancient Egyptian sky goddess of joy, love, music, and dance, and protector of women and family. In the

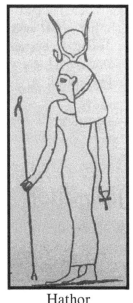
Hathor

ancient world she promised good husbands and wives to all who asked her for help. Visions of a future partner could be seen by those who scryed in her magical mirrors.

Hathor was allowed to see through the sacred eye of her father/consort Ra. In this way, she had knowledge of everything on the earth, in the sea, and in the heavens, and the thoughts as well as the deeds of humankind. Hathor also carried a shield that could reflect back all things in their true light.

From this shield, she fashioned the first magic mirror. One side was endowed with the power of Ra's eye (in other versions the power of the Eye of Horus, the young sky god) so that the seeker could see everything, no matter how distant in miles or how far into the future. The other side showed the gazer in his or her true light as they really were including strengths, weaknesses, and potentials.

The Mirror as a Universal Scrying Device

Though Hathor is associated with the origins of magical mirrors, they were consulted in ancient China, perhaps as early as 4000 C.E. to determine what would come to pass. These mirrors were believed to reflect the universe and give information about the stars and heavenly bodies.

Indeed, many practitioners mark their skill by the ability to *see* the surface of a mirror dissolve and move as water does, revealing its secrets from deep within the glass.

In the biblical Book of Enoch that was discovered as part of the Dead Sea Scrolls, the angel Azaziel taught humans to make magic mirrors. He did this so that so that distant scenes and people could be seen in them and that the scryers could receive guidance from the angels, much as the English astrologer Sir John Dee did in his crystal ball.

Merlin, King Arthur's magician, according to legend, used his magical mirror to warn the king about plots and potential invasions by enemy forces.

Mirrors and Love Divination

Though mirrors are used for all kinds of scrying in folk custom they have become associated with love in Eastern and Western Europe through the centuries. The custom traveled across the Atlantic and to the Southern hemisphere, where people of European origin settled, especially those with Celtic blood who were naturally regarded as having second or clairvoyant sight.

Typically, on one of the seasonal change points, a young unmarried girl would stand in candlelight at midnight or by the light of the full moon, in front of her mirror brushing her hair with 100 strokes.

As she gazed into the glass in a light trance, caused by the repetitious brushing movements at a time she was tired, the girl would call the image of an unknown lover into the glass with age old words passed down through the generations. This is just one version:

Mirror, mirror, send me

A vision pure and true

Of my lover waiting

Over seas so blue.

Beyond the tallest mountain,

Across the village street,

Come within the glass, my love

That we in truth may meet.

It was believed that, by seeing the image of a future love in the mirror, the scryer might even recognize the man as someone she already knew. However, if the girl saw the image of an unknown lover in the mirror, it was believed she would psychically draw him to her in the coming weeks. Of course, in more liberated times men can call their loves in the glass as well.

If the full moon rose on the evening before or the evening of a seasonal festival, the occasion was considered especially lucky for love divination. These occasions included:

- Halloween.

- Christmas Eve (or, in pre-Christian times the eve of the Midwinter Solstice, which fell around December 21st).

- New Year's Eve.

- Midsummer's Eve (in the Christian tradition, St. John's Eve, June 23rd or the older date, the evening before the Summer Solstice around June 21st).

- The saints days associated with love and marriage, St. Agnes Eve (January 20th) or the following night (the actual Saint's day). Agnes is the patron saint of virgins and betrothed couples.

- November 25th, the day and evening of the festival of St. Catherine of Alexandria, the fourth-century patron saint of young women, who was believed to bring good husbands to pure maidens.

- The evening before the festival of the Scottish love saint Andrew (November 29th)—or on the following night of St. Andrew's Day itself.

Mirrors and Folklore

Mirrors are sacred to the moon and water. Silver is the color and metal of the moon. If possible, obtain an old-fashioned mirror that contains silver in the glass, or a modern one backed with silver or in a silver frame. Round or oval mirrors are most often used for scrying. Monday, the day of the moon, is a favorable day for mirror scrying.

The Romans believed that if a mirror was broken, the soul of the person holding the mirror also shattered and it took seven years for the soul to grow again. This caused the superstition that breaking a mirror brought seven years of bad luck. The antidote was that you should wrap the broken mirror pieces in a piece of cloth and bury them deep where animals or children would not find them and cut themselves Some superstitions say it is unlucky to see the moon through or in glass but moonlight one of the most potent sources of scrying light, especially for love divination.

Should you capture the actual moon image in your mirror indoors or out, it is customary to say, "Father Moon, I would not hold you captive a moment longer than I need. Show me what I need to see, I ask you and then be on your way with my blessings." You can change the greeting if the moon is female in to you.

Preparing Your Mirror for Scrying

In medieval times, preparations for mirror scrying could be exacting with the chanting of angelic names, engraving seals of power in ancient alphabets, and blessing the mirror before scrying with fluid condensers, tinctures of gold, moonstone, and exotic herbs. You can still find details of how to make fluid condensers on the Internet.

If you buy a handmade magic mirror, these tinctures will have been applied during the making, and are also used to recharge a magick mirror or draw magical symbols on it.

Albertus Magnus, a German Dominican monk who was a philosopher, theologian, alchemist, and some say ceremonial magician, was born in 1208 and died in 1280. He described a process for preparing a new mirror for use by burying the scrying mirror at the crossroads on an odd number hour, leaving it for three days, digging it up, clearing the soil off, and showing an animal its reflection in the glass before using it.

Cleansing and Charging Your Mirror

If you want to make a formal cleansing and dedication of your mirror, use a pennyroyal herbal infusion that is just as effective as the fluid condensers and better for the glass. Pennyroyal is also used for blessing crystal balls. For dark mirrors, mugwort can be substituted (see next chapter). Hyssop infusion (*Hyssopus officinalis*) can also be used to cleanse any scrying tools including mirrors. If you cannot obtain either herb, use culinary sage (*Salvia*), the kind you buy in supermarkets in glass jars in the spices section, in the infusion.

First make your infusion. You can buy dried pennyroyal (*Mentha pulegium*) from a health store or via the Internet. It is a natural peace-bringing herb and also offers strength and protection. Alternatively, dry pennyroyal leaves from your garden and chop them very finely, or use the washed fresh chopped herb to make an infusion.

Use 1–2 teaspoons of the dried herb or 3 teaspoons of the fresh herb per cup, and 3 teaspoons of dried and 4 fresh per mug. Add boiling water to fill the cup or mug, stir, and cover. Leave for at least 10 minutes, strain off the herbs, and discard them. Stir the strained liquid again and leave it to cool. You can make some in advance and keep it bottled in the fridge for about a week. Alternatively, put the herbs in a small muslin bag in the cup/mug and then you do not need to strain.

The first time you use your mirror, place your infusion in a small bowl. Dip your index finger of the hand you write with into the liquid, in the center on the surface of the mirror. As large as you wish, draw a banishing pentagram for protection and cleansing, and then an attracting or invoking pentagram on top of it to empower your mirror. Be careful not to ingest anything from your finger.

Though associated with ritual magic the pentagram is an ancient spiritual symbol of the four Elements: Earth, Air, Fire, and Water rising to a fifth element made of the union of the other four. This is called Spirit, Aether, or Akasha and symbolizes Goddess energies.

Practice a few times until you can draw the pentagram both ways. The pentagram we are using is the Earth-based one, so it is very stable for spiritual work.

If this symbol is not right for you, draw an equal armed cross in the center of the mirror with the infusion and at the top of the cross say, "I ask the blessings of Uriel the transforming Archangel."

Bring the line down halfway, then on the right draw the horizontal line. At the right hand point saying, "I ask the blessings of Raphael the healing Archangel."

Draw the horizontal line across to the left and say, "I ask the blessings of Gabriel, Archangel of the Moon."

Take your finger back to the central vertical line and, moving down to the bottom point, say, "I ask the blessings of Michael, the Archangel of the Sun." Alternatively, draw the protective Eye of Horus/Ra on the mirror with infusion.

Eye of Horus

Then, polish the mirror with a clean, white, natural fabric cloth you keep for this purpose, asking for blessings on your work either from the powers of goodness and light, your Guardian Angel, the God/Goddess, a wise ancestor, the Lords (or Ladies) who guard time, or one of the deities suggested in Chapter 1.

Generally, before beginning mirror scrying you can draw the pentagrams, the cross, or the eye in front of the mirror in the air and then polish the mirror, asking for blessings on your work. You can at any time use the infusion as well.

Polish the mirror with clockwise movements to open it, and counterclockwise to close it down. Afterward, draw the pentagram, the cross, or the protective Eye of Horus/Ra on your mirror, either with your finger in the air or with infusion. Polish your mirror, giving thanks to whoever you called on for protection, and ask that you may use the knowledge wisely. Some practitioners cover the mirror with white cloth when not in use.

Noon sunlight is especially empowering for a clear glass mirror so it can be left uncovered in your scrying place if you wish. Do not expect to see an image as clear as a normal reflection when scrying, though some scryers do see a complete clear image almost instantly.

In fact, in this most elusive of psychic arts images may appear quite faint, sometimes as a light shimmer, at other times forming in a shadow, maybe an outline, or a gray formation, coming together in a black and white shape, and as quickly dissolving similar to wisps of mist, always fleeting.

On other occasions, the image can move in and out of vision, similar to the ripples clearing from water after a stone has been thrown. Some scryers complain the images will not stay still.

What you are left with it afterward is a strong impression in your mind, often more powerful than the images seen. You might think you saw nothing clearly, except you are left with this image that was released from the reflective mirror, which becomes very clear and vivid in your mind. However, some scryers see colors and quite powerful three-dimensional pictures in the glass over time. You will soon find your own way of *seeing*.

Opening Your Psychic Senses to Mirror Scrying

The best way to tune into mirror scrying if you are new to it is to go back to the technique we used in remote viewing in Chapter 1, called eidetic imagery, where you superimpose a detailed image on to a blank surface.

This skill is one associated with mirror scrying. In the early 1900s, Russian writer Maxim Gorky visited a Hindu holy man who showed him a book made of shining copper pages on which he could see pictures of Indian cities, temples, and the countryside. Then the wise man closed the book, blew on it, and showed Gorky the book again. The copper pages were blank. Gorky, a skeptic, was astonished. The guru was obviously so highly developed in spiritual arts that he was able to project his psychic visions on the reflective surface so that Gorky was able to see the pictures as though physical.

Practice with a clear mirror either in soft natural light or just before twilight with candles shining into it. Study a black-and-white photograph of a scene and memorize every detail. Black and white seems to work best while you are getting used to the technique.

Turn the photo over so you cannot see it , and look into the center of the mirror. Imagine the photograph building up on the surface of the mirror and gradually make it three-dimensional so it extends into the center of the mirror. Repeat with different photographs, but no more than one photograph per session.

When you are confident, choose an area in the mirror and with your eyes closed, imagine black-and-white images of people, places, and objects about which you have happy memories.

Open your eyes quickly, blink, and, as though you are taking a flashbulb photograph, project one of those happy images in a circle of light within the mirror as though casting a stone into a deep lake. Positive emotions create a strong psychic link.

Similar to ripples in the water, this image will come in and out of view. You may find it easier to have the mirror flat on the table while looking down into it and practicing.

When you are happy with this stage, think of a question, close your eyes, and imagine a totally empty mirror filling your mind. Then after a few seconds, open your eyes fast, blink, and project a circle of light from your mind into the mirror. You will *see* an image building in the glass that may be related to the issue you had been wondering about. Sometimes the image may appear and disappear several times or even change.

Now ask the same question with your eyes open. Focus on an area of light within the mirror and this time the image will build up as though seen through water drops. This may reveal a different, but related, image. Now let that image dissolve and another image appear. Continue until you have a number of images.

Do not worry about analyzing them for now unless you want to. When you can call up images in this way, you are ready for mirror scrying.

If difficult, go back to the last stage that worked and build up again. You have plenty of time, but if it seems unfruitful, try another form of scrying for a week or so and then return to your mirror.

These exercises will tune your clairvoyant powers into the mirror. Only practice for 10 minutes at first, then build it up to about 20 minutes at the last stage, changing the question whenever you wish, and allowing images to flow in and out of the glass.

Working With Clear Glass Mirrors

Soft sunlight during the early morning, later afternoon, or just before sunset, when red, pink, and purple light floods the mirror, are good for actual clear mirror scrying as opposed to practicing.

Generally mirrors are best for personal work, though, if you are working with a lover or family member, you can stand side by side gazing into a mirror to ask about a joint concern. You can also ask questions concerning others and how their decisions may affect your life.

Asking the question aloud after you have cleansed and empowered your mirror helps you to focus. You can ask further questions during the session. Generally 30 minutes is enough.

As well as being potent for bringing to the surface issues concerning personal identity and potential areas of personal and career development, mirror divination is effective for answering questions about fidelity, marriage, permanent love, relationships, fertility, and family concerns, and for discovering the location of an item or animal that is lost, or the truth about a matter that is hidden from you.

While scrying in a mirror, the surface may first move similar to water and ripple so you can see far within the mirror as though it was a deep pool. These deeper images may contain extra information concerning the more distant future as well as those secret worries and fears you perhaps have not expressed or formulated as questions.

If images do disappear too quickly, keep staring at the spot of light in the mirror where the image appeared and you will be able to re-create it in your mind and, as you become more experienced, call it back again into the glass. Some people only ever see the mirror images in their mind, and if you are one of those, use the mirror as a focus without worrying you are doing something wrong as the inner images will be just as accurate.

Incense sticks lit in front of or to the sides of the mirror will swirl upwards and help to soften the glass and make it seem more fluid.

Level 1
Working With Candles and Mirrors

This is the easiest form of mirror scrying, as candlelight is a potent source of images when reflected in the mirror. It is different from dark mirror scrying because you do not work in complete darkness and, of course, the clear mirror reflects more light. This method is also a good compromise if you do not like the idea of a dark mirror. You can try out some of the techniques I suggest in the following chapter

Work in semi-darkness, around sunset as twilight falls. Add extra candles around the room if it becomes dark outside quickly. Artificial light should not be used.

Candlelight scrying is similar to dark mirror scrying in that it is especially potent if carried out during the full moon period. If you angle your mirror to reflect moonbeams along with the candles, it will be at its highest strength. Use beeswax candles if possible. These release a gentle scent of honey and are the original scrying candles. If you cannot get beeswax, use white candles. A variety of shapes and sizes can create different light intensities and levels.

You can use either a large round or oval mirror on a wall or propped up on a table, a hand mirror with a handle, or a smaller tilting mirror on a stand. Place the candles in a semi-circle behind you or with a larger mirror (best for this kind of scrying) along the base of the mirror. Arrange the candles so you can see shafts of light interspersed with shadows. You may get shadows cast by other objects in the room, but make sure nothing reflects directly into the mirror. Experiment so that the effect becomes slightly other-worldly and magical, but not spooky.

Light the candles and an incense or oil of sandalwood, myrrh, jasmine, mimosa, carnation, or frankincense so the reflection of the smoke coils in the mirror. Prepare yourself by using one of the methods in Chapter 2 and sit or stand so that any ritual or blessing you carry out is reflected within the mirror and forms a dedication of the mirror. Then bless the mirrors I suggested earlier in this chapter.

Sit so that you are at the side of the mirror so you can see into it but do not see a reflection of your face. If working with a love partner or family member on a joint issue, the partner can sit on the opposite side of the mirror so that he or she can see in the mirror and maintain a counter-balance to your view.

Asking Questions

Ask a question very softly out loud and repeat it nine times, softer and softer until your voice is no more than a breath, and the last time is spoken as a whisper. Half-close your eyes and look first into the top right corner. This will tell you about the past.

You and any partner may see different images, as you are literally and symbolically viewing the situation from a different perspective. Use both of your images to see a joint path, and the reasons for the present situation or dilemma that may be rooted in your separate pasts.

Pass your hands in front of the mirror in counterclockwise circles, palms toward it, to clear away the past impressions. Alternatively, slowly blow three times onto the surface and with, the hand you write with, make a single sweeping movement left to right, top to bottom, a few centimeters in front of the glass and say, "Blessings be on this wise mirror."

Close your eyes for a moment. Open them again slowly and focus on the center of the mirror to see the present issue. This may be different from what you thought it was, and it may reveal unexpected opportunities, help, or opposition. With mirror scrying, the interpretation is strongly based in what you feel about the images.

Clear the mirror again by passing your hands in circles or by blowing gently a few centimeters in front of it. Close your eyes again and, as you open them, look into the far top left of the mirror and see what is coming into your life. Extinguish the candles and you may obtain a final image to link the three stages in the momentary afterglow in the mirror.

When you have finished, you can ask your Guardian Angel (or Spirit Guide) to appear in the glass. If you relax and half-close your eyes while focusing on a pool of light, you may see his or her reflection in the glass.

At first these may be just glimpses, but even if the image fades, focus on the same place of light in the mirror where the guardian appeared. He or she may emerge again in the same spot and a message of guidance comes into your mind (see also the next chapter).

You can also use this method for daytime clear mirror scrying.

Level 2
Working With Hathor Mirrors

Hathor mirrors were originally small, hand-mirror size, round and double-sided, and made of polished silver, copper, or bronze on both sides with a wooden or bone handle, and an image of Hathor on the handle. The idea of this was that, as you looked at your own image in the mirror, she was beneath it supporting you so you would not be afraid, especially when looking at yourself in your true light.

Ordinary Egyptian women kept a Hathor mirror on the family altar surrounded by small turquoise crystals to keep it pure. They would mirror gaze in the hour before sunset so the red and pink rays were reflected in the mirror and would ask her about matters concerning the house and home, and about the future of their children born or unborn. Hathor mirrors are good for answering questions about all matters concerning home and family, love partnerships and relationships of all kinds, and fertility and children, as well as ones about personal identity and self-esteem. They were also used by midwives and priests after the birth of a child to make forecasts about the little one's potential, and also to ask Hathor to choose the right name for the child. You can buy Hathor mirrors on the Internet by mail order.

Hathor's special time for scrying is the hour before sunset, and the luckiest month is Hathor's special month that ran from September 17th to October 16th known as Athyr. The first day is her festival and luckiest of all for using your Hathor mirror.

Her direction is West—the direction of the setting sun—and she was said to guide the deceased into the Otherworld and rebirth them through a gate on the Western horizon. For this reason, Hathor is often called Lady of the West. If possible, sit in the West facing the mirror so it will reflect the rays of the sunset if you have a window behind you or are outdoors. However, you can also scry in soft sunlight or natural light. If you are not working with the sunset, sit facing a plain wall.

You can adapt a small, plain, highly polished silver or copper-colored tray if you wish to try scrying with metal. Most people, however, use clear glass. You can buy clear, double-sided swivel mirrors, the kind intended for putting on makeup or shaving, and so you have a magnifying effect on one side. You may be able to get a three-sided mirror from a garage sale or antique market. These can also be used for candle and mirror scrying.

Red, pink, or orange candles (Hathor's colors) are lit on either side of the mirror at any time of day so their flickering light helps to evoke psychic images. Rose incense, the incense of Hathor, is also burned to stimulate the psychic senses, or you can place a vase of fragrant roses or rose-based potpourri near the mirror.

Small turquoise or malachite crystals, or small items of gold, such as earrings, circling the mirror are traditionally the crystals and metal of Hathor. They will help to empower your mirror work.

Cleanse and empower your Hathor mirror by drawing the Eye of Horus on the surface in pennyroyal or hyssop, or with your finger in the air in front of it. Polish with a white cloth or, if you prefer, rose pink.

Ask the blessings of Hathor or your own mother deity figure (see Chapter 1 for suggested chants if you want to make the ceremony more formal). If you have a single-sided mirror, you will look for two images, one after the other.

The first image or first side of the mirror will reveal how you can attain a particular dream or ambition, or resolve a current dilemma that is holding you back from happiness or fulfillment. You will *see* yourself carrying out an action, or perhaps another person or event intervening to bring the desired result. This will act as a guide in the weeks or months ahead so you know the steps to take or people to approach.

The second image, or other side of the mirror, shows yourself in your true light, both as you are now and as you can become. For me, this is the single most important piece of information in any form of scrying. Often, we lack self-belief and confidence because others in the past have criticized or diminished us. Although great Pharaohs were afraid to see their true selves in Hathor's mirror because they would see their own weaknesses, most ordinary people find when they look into the mirror of Hathor that they are far more attractive, charismatic, and talented than they believed possible. This self-knowledge and increased self-esteem mean that the prophecy revealed in the first image is more likely to be fulfilled, because we are suddenly more open to embracing opportunities and new people.

For the first image or side of the mirror, sit or stand so that you cannot see yourself within it. If one side of the mirror magnifies, use it for this question. Stare hard into the mirror, close your eyes, open them, and blink rapidly. In that second of intensity and altered vision, the image will appear in the mirror when you blink and will build up before gradually fading.

Continue to look through relaxed, half-closed eyes at the same place in the mirror and the original image may come back into focus before fading again. The impressions or words in your mind expand the meaning of what you have seen.

Now turn the mirror over or, if using the same side, blow on it or pass your hands in front of it in circles counterclockwise, as I described in the section on candle and mirror scrying. Next, stand or sit so that you can see yourself or at least your face in the mirror. Smile and relax. Take time to study and reflect on your actual physical image and focus only on your positive attributes and talents.

Very slowly close your eyes and open them equally as slow. Picture yourself framed in soft radiance and become aware of yourself as you could become. You will still be yourself, not necessarily 10 pounds thinner or with a different hairstyle, unless that is what you want. But you will be in glowing health, with eyes that shine with happiness and a smile that is not forced.

Even if the image is only fleeting, continue looking at your reflection as it is now, and it will subtly change as your aura or energy field brightens and shines ever more radiantly within the mirror, especially around your head and face.

The image of yourself as you really are may become steady as you continue to gaze. Confidence and self-love will grow and merge with your physical external self.

You will become aware of the inner person within you behind the layers of wife, mother, daughter, and employer/employee. You will know you are special, that you are worthy of love and respect, and can ask it of others.

Perhaps you wish to loosen some of the ties that restrict you or overcome fears of being lonely if you leave a less-than-satisfactory relationship.

As you gaze, you will become aware of yourself in the home you choose for the future, which may be your present one if you love it. It may be different, in another town, or even in another country if that is what you dream of. You may see yourself having turned an interest or gift into a business or career or cutting back on a successful yet stressful life to raise a family or grow flowers.

When you feel the connection fading, cleanse your mirror and thank Hathor for her support. Do not be in too much of a hurry to rejoin the world.

Repeat the Hathor mirror scrying regularly—monthly at least—and you will find that the new self becomes more evident in your everyday world.

Interpreting Images

These can also be applied to Water or crystal ball scrying. Earlier I described how if you are doing a past, present, and future three-image reading, the top right represents the past, the center represents the present, and the top left the future.

Some practitioners divide the mirror into three imaginary vertical sections such as invisible stripes, right top to bottom for the past, center top to bottom for the present, and left top to bottom for the future.

However, for general mirror work where you are not limiting the number of images you look for, the following, more detailed rules may prove helpful. See which system works for you, as there are slight differences in emphasis. These rules, similar to all others, are based on what people have found works for them, but you should make your own rules according to what feels right to you.

- An image moving towards the scryer suggests that the event or person suggested by a specific image will occur or appear very soon in the scryer's life.

- An image moving away suggests that the event or person signified by the image is either moving away from the scryer's world or that a past issue or relationship may still be exerting undue influence on the scryer.

- Images appearing on the left of the mirror suggest actual physical situations or encounters that may influence or change your life in the near future.

- Images appearing in the center or to the right tend to be symbolic.

- Pictures near the top of the mirror are regarded as especially significant and need prompt attention.

- ✍ Those in the corners or at the bottom are less prominent or urgent.

- ✍ The relative size and clarity of the images can indicate their importance.

- ✍ Images that change into another reflect that the next stage is coming fast into your life or that they are closely linked.

- ✍ A scene rather than an image that appears signifies that a number, people, or factors will soon be influencing your immediate world.

- ✍ A fleeting image that fills the mirror says that you, and not others, need to be center stage in your priorities and that you should take the lead or speak out.

- ✍ If you get a scene of people in unfamiliar clothes or locations it may be a past world.

- ✍ It is a good sign to see people you know well and this says you should contact them even if he or she lives far away as they are thinking strongly of you. Or they may welcome your support right now. If it is an old lover, he or she may be coming back into your life or would like to.

- ✍ Seeing a deceased relative in a mirror is a way of saying his or her love is still with you, and you may have a momentary glimpse of him or her happy in the afterlife (see also dark mirror work).

- ✍ Regularly seeing people you do not know suggests evolving mediumship abilities, but you do not have to develop these unless you wish to or feel ready.

- ✍ If you are unattached, seeing an unknown person and sensing love means that this unknown person is contacting you telepathically and you may meet before long.

Chapter 11

Dark Mirror Scrying

Scrying in dark glass mirrors and dark bowls is wrongly regarded as a medium in which bad spirits or fearsome ghosts may be seen. This B-movie hype is fueled by old magical Grimoire, a collection of spells and practices usually from medieval times. These were written by practitioners whose Latin names claim connection with lost wisdom from a thousand years earlier, and who were very concerned with manipulating spirit powers.

Dark is synonymous with the unknown and therefore the feared, and with black magic and earth. This is purely a Western concept, and in a number of indigenous cultures such as the Australian Aborigines, parts of sub-Saharan Africa, and native North America, death and spirits are associated with yellow or white rather than black.

In Chinese tradition, the black yin is the female nurturing part and necessary polarity for the white yang. For without darkness, there can be no awareness of light, without night no day, and without rest no restoration. Indeed, in the symbol the seeds of the one are contained in the other forming the whole.

Yin/Yang

In the ancient Egyptian tradition, black is linked with *kmt* or *kemet*, which means "the black land." Kemet was one of the names for Egypt, referring to the rich silt deposited by the Nile Flood, in which the crops grew. Therefore, black was primarily a color of fertility and rebirth. Life, they believed, originally came from the dark primordial waters.

It also was the color of the Underworld and specifically of Osiris, the underworld and rebirth father god who caused the constant cycle of regeneration and was instrumental in giving the blessed dead rebirth.

Therefore, dark scrying with mirrors and bowls is a very beautiful and spiritual form of scrying. It makes it possible for us to work with spiritual realms and our own spirituality, and to uncover and overcome our sometimes-unacknowledged fears of the unknown.

Of course, people who fool around with dark mirrors, calling spirits into them and using old words they do not understand from some dubious Internet demonology tract, are going to get their minds into all kinds of trouble. It is no different than opening your front door in the center of a city at midnight and inviting anyone who would like to party to come in.

But dark scrying is not for everyone, and, if you do not feel ready, it is not right for you. Read this chapter and work with one of the many other methods in this book that feels more in tune with your needs and personality.

Dark Mirrors in Magical Tradition

Dark mirrors are often called witches' mirrors because many practitioners of Witchcraft do possess one for scrying and for talking to their special Witch Guardian, who guides their magical learning.

But whatever religious persuasion or lack thereof, dark mirrors are an excellent way of creating gateways into other worlds as well as answering questions about your inner and spiritual world.

What you see in a dark mirror may appear to be a grainy black-and-white still photograph or, alternatively, similar to an old-fashioned black-and-white silent film where the images flicker intensely. Though you may see colors in clear mirrors, these are very rare in dark ones.

Dark Mirrors in the Ancient World

Remains of Central American Mayan temples have shown dark transparent obsidian-like slabs on a pedestal in small round temple buildings, as well as obsidian mirrors on some walls. The Incas of Peru in South America also consulted dark mirrors. There is also a lesser tradition of obsidian being used for scrying in native North America.

The Aztecs have the strongest tradition for obsidian mirrors. If you can obtain a shimmering rainbow obsidian either as a mirror or a sphere, this is the most perfect scrying material (though not cheap).

Obsidian was sacred to the Sky God Tezcatlipoca, and was used in scrying mirrors and to observe eclipses. Through his obsidian mirror, Tezcatlipoca could see all that occurred within the world and the heavens.

Obsidian was used symbolically in the eyes of statues in the Temple of the God of the Winds and Sun, Quetzalcoatl, to symbolize the all-seeing eye of the God even in the darkness.

Tezcatlipoca was the god most associated with obsidian mirrors. His name means "smoking mirror" and it was said that, similar to Hathor's mirror, it reflected the true nature of any who looked in it, as well as giving visions of the future. Refer back to Chapter 10 on Hathor mirror magick for details on how to carry out this technique in dark mirrors.

Tezcatlipoca was Lord of the Aztec Gods and supreme Sun God of the First Sun, as well as a god of the dark sun as it crossed the Mictlan (the Underworld) each night. In this form, the god became a black jaguar because of its fierceness and ability to see in the dark.

He was also god of magick and mystery, akin to the Roman god of the Underworld, Pluto. During one battle, Tezcatlipoca's foot was cut off when his rival and nephew Quetzalcoatl slammed the gates of heaven on it. The foot was replaced with a foot carved from pure obsidian, through which he could see the world and the intentions of others.

Tezcatlipoca had his revenge when Quetzalcoatl looked into the obsidian mirror and saw himself not as the great god he believed he was, but as a feathered serpent. This caused him to leave the Aztec world in shame.

Choosing or Making Your Dark Mirror

The finest example of a dark witch mirror I have seen was in the Museum of Witchcraft at Boscastle in Cornwall in the UK. It has a wooden frame carved into the face of a witch. At the time of this writing, it is displayed on the Museum's Website.

Your dark mirror should, if possible, be made of darkened smoky glass (the kind you see on tinted windows for cars). These look almost opaque until candlelight shines in them. You can buy them on the Internet and one that's the size of an average closed book is large enough.

Best of all are obsidian mirrors though these are quite expensive, unless you choose a small one, but they are fabulous for serious scryers. You can alternatively buy mirrors made from the same material as black, shiny wall tiles or improvise and frame a black tile.

You can make your own dark mirrors quite easily. Maria, a woman I met at a festival in Wales recently, described how she made a dark mirror by placing a shiny black card into a picture frame so it fitted exactly. She then put plain glass in front of the card.

Alternatively, spray or brush with black enamel paint on the back of a sheet of clear glass from an empty picture frame. Put the clear unpainted glass to the front so the black shines through and return it to the frame.

Ensure that the glass is spotlessly clean before you add the paint. The secret is to spray or brush a single, light coat of paint over the glass and let it dry completely before adding the next layer, letting that dry, and so on until no light shines through when the glass is held up to the light. Leave to dry as long as necessary.

Caring for and Keeping Your Dark Mirror

Dark mirrors, unlike dark bowls, should not be exposed to sunlight, though moonlight is good. Indeed, leave your dark mirror uncovered on the night of the full moon to empower it, whether or not the rays of the moon fall upon it.

Mugwort infusion is generally used for cleaning a dark mirror when you first acquire it and then before and after each use.

Some practitioners also scatter mugwort herb on their scrying table in front of the mirror, as it is believed to enhance psychic powers and make the transition to higher states of awareness easier.

Mugwort (*Artemisia vulgaris*) is easily obtainable as a dried herb from health stores and on the Internet. The leaves are generally used for an infusion (if you dry your own herbs from the garden). Mugwort is also soothing for digestion and inducing relaxation, and some practitioners drink warm mugwort infusion before scrying. However, it should not be taken during pregnancy, and I would advise caution in drinking herbal remedies unless you talk to a practitioner or are experienced in herbalism.

For a cleansing infusion or for drinking as a tea, pour an average-sized cup of boiling water into a bowl containing 1–2 teaspoons of the dried herb. For a mug size you would use 3 teaspoons of the herb. For quickness, you can put the herb in the bottom of the mug and add the boiling water. Stir, cover, and leave to infuse for at least 10 minutes, strain off the herb, and leave the infusion to cool. Except for the first cleansing, you will only need a very small amount, so you can keep some ready and bottled in the refrigerator.

The first time you use your dark mirror, lay it flat and sprinkle mugwort infusion on the surface. Say, "Be blessed and be cleansed of all that is not pure and good." Then wipe it dry with a soft cloth kept especially for that purpose, and afterward wash and dry. Say, "Be blessed and be filled with love and kindness."

Finally, polish the mirror with a small piece of very soft, dark, natural fabric such as silk, again kept solely for the mirror, saying, "I give thanks to those who guard and watch over my mirror and my work with it."

Before and after scrying, you only need to sprinkle the mirror with a few drops of infusion, dry, and polish, saying the words as above.

You can use the same infusion before and after scrying and then throw it away outdoors or under running water.

Before beginning, you can use the infusion to anoint the center of your hairline, the center of you brow, your throat, and your two inner wrist points, your four higher chakra points. These will automatically activate and protect the lower ones(see pages 38–40). Be sure to spot-test first to make sure you aren't allergic.

Afterward, anoint them again in reverse order to close the energies (use clear water if you are pregnant).

For crystal ball and clear mirror scrying you did not dry the ball, but just polished it after sprinkling. For dark mirrors the extra stage seems effective, but you can combine drying and polishing, and the second and third chants if you prefer.

Cleansing by Smudging

If your mirror is very expensive (for example, made of obsidian), you can use a cedar or sagebrush smudge (herbal smoke stick) for the cleansing stage and then polish it with a soft cloth.

Light the smudge and, when the flame dies down, blow on it gently until it glows red. Then, holding it your power hand (the one you write with), begin by smudging all around your head and shoulders, down your body, and around your heart and both hands and arms. Use alternating spirals of smoke to activate and protect your higher charkas.

Then swirl the smoke three times around the mirror counterclockwise, reciting the first cleansing chant, and then three times clockwise, saying the second set of words. Finally, polish the mirror as before using the third chant. You can substitute a cedar, sage, or pine incense stick.

You can leave the smudge or incense burning in the background during the scrying session(see the following section) and afterwards to close your higher charkas. If necessary, light a new smudge. You only need to use a mini-sized smudge for cleansing.

Working With a Dark Mirror

You can scry in a darkened mirror as you would for a clear mirror, using candles for illumination. However, this is not their traditional usage.

According to Cecil Williamson, the original collector of many of the items now in the UK Boscastle Witchcraft Museum, dark mirrors could form a home for one's familiar spirit.

This entity is equivalent to your Spirit Guide who assists you with spiritual work, and is often someone who, in his or her own lifetime, was involved in spiritual matters, whether as a herbalist, a wise man or woman, a priest or priestess from a pre-Christian tradition, or even a traditionally religious monk or nun.

In this old tradition, the figure of the Guide would be seen reflected in the darkened glass as you looked into it, standing behind you. You could talk to the shadowy person reflected there, who would help, teach, and advise you, but according to folk custom you must never turn around or the Guardian would disappear.

Of course if you do not believe in Spirit Guides, this person would be equated with your own evolved spiritual self whom your mind was projecting as an external figure behind you. Whatever your belief, the following method uses the same principles:

✍ In your scrying place, hang your dark mirror on a wall away from windows or doors that might illuminate it. Alternatively, prop a smaller dark mirror on a table or flat surface so you can see into it while sitting.

✍ Some practitioners cover the mirror in dark silk when not in use, just as some wrap their smaller clear scrying mirrors in white silk.

✍ If using a larger mirror on the wall, put a tall narrow table or shelf in front of it so that you can position a pair of tall white candles to shine into the glass as you stand looking into it, making a doorway of faint light.

✍ Unlike the method for clear mirrors, stand or sit so you can see your own reflection in the dark glass unless you prefer not to. By seeing yourself you are setting your spiritual inner self within the mirror and opening yourself to seeing other dimensions.

- ✍ The room should be dark except for the candles.

- ✍ You can make a pathway of candles on the table— two or three small white ones in a vertical row so they reflect within the mirror into the darkness. This can form a wonderful pathway to past worlds or other dimensions, especially after a session of meditation.

- ✍ Cast a protective circle of light around yourself and the glass before scrying. Do this by making a circle in the air below shoulder level, with a clear quartz crystal point as you face the mirror, so the circle is made at the same time in the mirror. Do this immediately after lighting the candles.

- ✍ Say, "May only goodness and light remain within this circle as I work only for good and with the purest intent."

- ✍ Light protective incense, such as rose, myrrh, or lavender, so the reflection of the smoke swirls in the glass. If you already have used incense or smudge for cleansing the mirror, you can substitute this.

- ✍ Hold or set in front of you on the table a protective crystal such as smoky quartz, rutilated quartz, or amethyst if you wish.

Seeing the Wise Ones in the Mirror

Close your eyes and ask that you may see or sense the kindly presence of your Spirit Guide who helps you on your spiritual journey, a wise ancestor or teacher, or your Guardian Angel. You are not calling up spirits, but an image of them in their world—nothing can come out of the glass.

You can either specify whom you would like to see or say, "Whoever is right for me to see to best guide me at this point of time." You may encounter a new guide or angel during the session who may take the place of the first figure.

Open your eyes slowly. At this time, you may see or feel a gentle-loving, shadowy presence standing behind you and be filled with love and peace. Do not turn around.

Ask if he or she has a message or teaching for you; the words will flow into your mind. You can, if you have a specific question, no matter how mundane it is, ask it now. There is no point in trying to receive higher wisdom if you are worried sick about buying new tires for the car or paying your child's college fees. A solution may come into your mind or you may see a grainy, black-and-white image in the glass that will make perfect sense, either immediately or in the hours after scrying.

When you are ready, thank the Guardian or whoever has appeared and say, "Go in peace and in blessings until we meet again."

Close your eyes. When you open them do not look into the glass but blow out the candles one by one; sit and enjoy the fragrance. When you are ready, cleanse the mirror, and then anoint or smudge yourself in the incense smoke by spiraling it around you clockwise and counterclockwise. Leave it to burn through.

In the unlikely event you ever you feel afraid while using a dark mirror or find it hard to break the connection even with a loving guardian, say, "Blessings be," blow out the candles fast one after the other and then say, "Go in peace. I remain myself and separate. So shall it be," and smudge yourself in the incense smoke or anoint your higher chakras.

You will not have called anything bad nor can your spirit get trapped in the glass. However, occasionally there are times when earthly matters naturally cloud our mind and we can project our fears into the glass in ways that may frighten us.

Answering Questions With a Dark Mirror

You do not have to work with Spirit Guides but can use your dark mirror to answer a question about something that is not clear—something that you feel is being kept from you by someone in your everyday life or about the more distant future. You can also use it to discover the location of what has been lost or what has happened to someone you used to know.

As well as your pair of doorway candles, light a pathway of small candles vertically across the table towards the mirror so they reflect within the mirror into the darkness. This is a wonderful pathway to past worlds or other dimensions, as well as to focus yourself for answering questions.

This time sit at the side of the mirror rather than being reflected in it so you can see the pathway of light within the mirror. Breathe gently and regularly, and picture the mirror surface rippling and dissolving similar to water so you can walk through the doorway of light. You may experience a slight inner sensation as you enter the mirror in your mind, but this is very gentle. Only your mind is exploring the mirror and you cannot get stuck inside.

At the far end of the light pathway deep in the mirror, visualize a second doorway of pure light that swings open. Look through the doorway before it closes and you will see either a symbol offered to you by unseen hands that will answer your question, or a fleeting scene that will show you what is missing or link you with the person you seek to contact. It seems that such scrying may actually activate telepathic links and the person may contact you.

When you have these answers retrace steps in your mind back along the light path through the mirror to the everyday world. Thank your wise guardians who have protected you, cleanse, and polish your mirror, and then blow out the candles one after the other.

Reading the Words of the Future

When you have been using it for a while, a black mirror will become a doorway into the astral plane along the same candle pathway. This time you will see through the inner doorway a shining, gold-covered book—the Akashic Records—of wisdom and experience of humans past, present, and future

The book will open and you may *see* words of light in the mirror or just a shimmering as though the mirror is filled with the huge book of light. You will hear the words or see them in your mind. This will give you important information about future directions you could take and unexpected opportunities.

Calling the Presence of a Loved One Who Has Died

For some people, dreaming of a deceased love one or sensing his or her peaceful presence is enough. But for others, *seeing* the relative and knowing he or she is now well and happy is part of the grieving process, especially if the last days were traumatic or you were unable to say goodbye. A relative would never spook you, but if you don't want to *see* the relative, then don't try the following ritual, as it is very powerful.

The use of mirrors and candles to connect with the dead is common to many ages and cultures. The Romans believed that when we looked in a mirror we could see our soul, and so the superstition grew that breaking mirrors was bad luck.

Until about 50 years ago, mirrors were covered in the home after a person died so that their soul would be able to fly free and not remain caught in the glass. Fortunately, not many people believe in that superstition anymore.

You are not capturing the soul of your relative in the glass, but using the reflective surface to allow you to perceive and to amplify his or her presence through your clairvoyant eye.

Use genuine beeswax candles if possible, as these release a gentle scent of honey and are the original candles used for this purpose.

Generally, 10 p.m. is called the Healing hour. It is a good time for this kind of mirror work, but any after dusk period will be good, especially during the waning moon (check your diary or the weather page of a newspaper).

Polish the mirror with your soft cloth before use or use the three stages of cleansing if you wish. However, ask at each stage that your loved one may reveal him- or herself in love as he or she is called by you now and remembered with love. Use mugwort rather than smudge, because the former is a little heavy for this purpose.

Recall the image of your relative in your mind as you polish the mirror, picturing him or her carrying out a favorite relax-ing occupation, such as gardening, reading, or playing music. Light rose incense sticks (the fragrance of Hathor), and also a fragrance of gentle family love.

Work in candlelight, and use three candles positioned in a triangular shape so that one is facing directly into the mirror but furthest away from it, forming the apex of the triangle. The other two candles marking the ends of the triangle of light should be placed close to the mirror at the left and right sides, near to the edges of the frame. You should be able to see all three candles in the mirror.

It is said that the space directly in front of the apex candle within the mirror is the gateway to the other dimensions. Ancient magicians did very complex measurements to align the apex candle on a North/South axis to the Pole Star. But because we want to see Grandma or Grandpa and not Infinity in the glass, we don't need to be so precise.

Sit or stand so that you can see the center of the glass but your own reflection cannot be seen in the mirror. Some people look directly into the mirror so that the face of the loved one overlays their own reflection. Spend time watching the shadows and light flickering in the glass and letting patterns of light and darkness form in the mirror. This is the backcloth of the image you hope to receive.

The secret of this kind of mirror work is to relax. Don't stare too hard, but with half-closed eyes. If you want to close your eyes momentarily, do so. Think of your relative with affection and focus on special private moments you shared.

Breathe very gently and regularly, and visualize the light converging in the center of the mirror as light beams. Then, very slowly and gently, close your eyes. If you relax there will appear an image of your loved one in black and white, gray, and deep blue, similar to a silhouette on a screen in your mind. The person may appear younger and surrounded by light.

At this point, open your eyes as slowly as possible, as if you are waking from a long sleep into a brightly lit room. Blink if you want to. You may momentarily glimpse the shadowy silhouette image of your loved one against the light frame in the center of the mirror. At first the image in the mirror may be quite misty but will be instantly recognizable. Look for no longer than half a minute at the mirror image.

Close your eyes slowly again and refocus on the image in your mind. It will be a brighter and clearer version of the one in the mirror, but still in gray, blue, and black and white. The visions have been described as being similar to those seen on very old, silent, black-and-white films of the 1920s and 1930s.

Very slowly reopen your eyes and you may see the image more clearly in the glass, but still in silhouette and flickering. Continue four or five times, each time closing your eyes after looking in the mirror at the image for half a minute.

Eventually, you may be rewarded by a smile and a more distinct image on the screen in your mind, or, if you are lucky, the mirror, though almost always still in silhouette shades. At this point you may hear the well-loved voice in your mind and know that the loved one is well and happy.

If you have anything to say—love, regrets, or unfinished business—speak now and you will know that your words have been accepted. Close your eyes and thank the presence. When you open them do not look into the mirror, for the image will be gone.

Blow out the candles one by one in any order you like and, for each, send a message of love to your departed relation. Above all, give him or her permission to go on to where he or she will be happy, knowing that love never dies. This can be very liberating if guilt was an issue in life.

Finally, sit quietly in the dark absorbing the incense fragrance. When you are ready, switch on the lights and cleanse and polish the mirror again. Spend the rest of the evening with family or, if alone in the house, reading or carrying out some routine physical task until bedtime. You may dream of your loved one. Carry out the ritual no more than once a month.

If you do feel afraid at any stage, say, "Go in peace and with my love and blessings. I thank you for your presence, but I am not yet ready to continue the connection. But the love is there between us forever."

Then close your eyes, and when you open them the image should have gone. If not, blow out the candles and switch on the light. Have a bath in rose or lavender to relax yourself and do some physical activity to bring you back down to earth, such as eating a light meal.

Dark Mirrors and Moonlight

Though I have said that it is best not to have your dark mirror where light from windows and doors shines on it, full moonlight is good for empowering your mirror and also for a special kind of scrying. So you can move your mirror on the night of the full moon to where the light will shine within it.

Calling Down the Moon Energies

In pre-Christian times and still in modern Witchcraft, the moon goddess Diana, the Roman full moon mother goddess Selene (known for her many children), the wise woman Hecate, who stands at the triple crossroads where past, present, and future meet or numerous other lunar goddesses, are called on the night of the full moon to empower practitioners and inspire them with prophetic wisdom.

When the moon is shining brightly, take your mirror out-doors and set it on the ground, on a waterproof surface to pro-tect the back of the mirror. Cleanse it with just a few drops of still mineral water and then dry and polish it, saying as you sprinkle the water, "I seek the wisdom of the moon." As you polish it, say, "I seek the healing blessings of the moon 'and as you polish it' I seek the enlightenment of the moon and so give blessings to the moon and all who stand or sleep beneath her rays."

Around your mirror put a clockwise circle of small moon-stones or clear glass nuggets. Walk in a circle around the mirror, making a soft continuous empowerment, such as, "Call down the moon, call down the power, reveal in the mirror, and the truth at this hour."

You can create your own chant to repeat or work in silence. When you have circled the mirror nine times clockwise, the number of perfection, stop and spin on the spot, very fast until you feel dizzy.

Look up at the moon and you will feel it rushing towards you, a physiological response, but one that creates a psychic connection opening your prophetic powers. Sit down, steady yourself, and look straight into the moonlit dark mirror. You will usually see a picture or maybe a series of fast images and at the same time words will flow in your mind that will expand the horizons of possibility for you.

Then close your eyes and, when you look again in the mirror ask what it is that you most want to know. The images and words will continue to flow. When you are finished, splash just a few drops of water on the mirror and leave them to dry naturally.

Sit quietly in the moonlight and, when you are ready collect the moonstones counterclockwise, pick up your mirror and say, "May I walk always in the beauty and light of the moon. Blessings be on all."

This really only works when the moon is shining so save this for good weather. If you can stay warm, you can work in winter, especially in snow, sitting on warm blankets on top of a waterproof covering.

Scrying With Dark Bowls

Dark bowl and water scrying is very effective for uncovering secrets, revealing the truth of a matter, and finding out who are unexpected allies or people who may be less than helpful, whatever they say. It is also good for health matters and for discovering an unknown lover, or the intentions of someone you really like, but of whose feelings you are uncertain.

You can buy matte black basalt, marble, or onyx scrying bowls, or stone or ceramic ones with a dark inner lining from New Age outlets everywhere. You can also use dark crystal bowls. However, you can also visit your local store and see smoked glass bowls or black shiny ceramic ones. The bowl need not be large unless you are working for a group.

Cleanse the bowl when you first acquire it by partly filling it with cooled mugwort infusion, and swirling it three times counterclockwise, three times clockwise, and three times counterclockwise again, saying, "Be be cleansed of all doubt or negativity and reveal the truth clearly, but with kindness and with compassion, this I ask."

Swirl it three more times clockwise repeating the same words to empower it and then pour the infusion outdoors on to earth or, if not possible, under a running tap.

Alternatively, you can partly fill the bowl with either dried lavender or dried rose petals, swirl, and speak the empowerment, then pour the petals outdoors on to the ground or from an open window. I suggest you look back at the water scrying section, as the techniques are very similar.

You can scry by candlelight so it shines directly on to the water. I use a horseshoe of small candles at the back of the bowl.

Some people prefer the candlelight at the sides rather than directly in the water, so experiment.

Work in moonlight any time when the waxing moon is bright enough to illuminate the water. Best of all is the night of the full moon, as well as or instead of using your magick mirror. Alternatively, work in bright sunlight outdoors so the light ripples the water.

I sometimes add a drop or two of a yellow oil, such as sunflower or olive oil to the water especially in sunlight (see Chapter 8 for more on oil scrying).

Swirl the bowl of water three times clockwise, three times counterclockwise, and three times clockwise before beginning, while reciting the question softly over and over again. Then stare hard into the illuminated water and, especially if you have used a little oil, images of light will form within the dark bowl. Look deep inside the water rather than on the surface.

When you have finished, say, "May I use these insights wisely and gently to harm none, least of all myself. Blessings be on all."

Swirl the water nine times as you did before starting, and pour the water out on the ground if possible. That is sufficient cleansing. Allow the bowl to dry naturally and put it away wrapped in a dark, natural piece of cloth or a drawstring bag if small enough.

You will usually receive confirmation of what you learned in the days ahead.

Chapter 12

Scrying With Crystal Balls

In this chapter I will focus on using clear quartz crystal spheres that are the best for scrying. I will also describe working with others transparent or semi-transparent crystals, such as amethyst. I will also deal with opaque spheres and eggs, along with shadow scrying in Chapter 14.

Because crystal balls are perfect spheres, they have no beginning and no end. They reflect a miniature cosmos, acting as a bridge between human and spiritual realms. Sixteenth-century alchemist and philosopher Paracelsus (1493–1541) believed that because the crystal ball belonged to the Element of Air, anything under or within the heavens could be seen within it. (I have mentioned one of his books in the Useful Reading section.)

Clear crystal quartz has been called the "essence" or "breath of the dragon" in China and Japan, "visible nothingness" by Buddhists, and "frozen light" in ancient Greece. The original crystal of truth, according to Greek legend, was thrown by Hercules from Mount Olympus. It shattered into millions of smaller crystals. Some rolled down the mountainside and became spheres. It is said you will always see the truth within a crystal sphere.

What Kind of Crystal Ball Should You Use?

If you have only one crystal ball, it should be clear, natural quartz crystal—not manufactured lead crystal or glass. Real quartz has markings inside that look to be cracks and can be used for any form of clairvoyant work.

Balls with inclusions and sparkling rainbows within allow the physical eye to lead the spiritual eye inwards to psychically interpret these outwardly visible images.

Clear crystal spheres also provide a focus for angel and Spirit Guide communication. And in meditation, they enable a scryer to walk through crystal pathways in the ball into past realms and other dimensions. They can also be used for amplifying and transmitting healing rays to those who are sick, even if they are far from the scryer, by picturing the image of the person well and strong as the ball is held up to sun or moonlight.

You need not buy a very expensive crystal sphere, but it should be, if possible, the size of an average orange so you have sufficient depth and a variety of crystalline markings to stimulate clairvoyance. A good-quality, clear quartz crystal ball is an investment that acts as a centerpiece for all your clairvoyant work and to energize your scrying place.

Choose one with inner markings that are not just dense masses but with different intensities of crystal formations to allow the eye to weave in and out. Balls made of other kinds of crystal can be slightly smaller but also need transparent areas and markings within it to guide the eyes to perceive the images.

Crystal balls need some illumination, though this can be quite subtle. Some practitioners working indoors prefer dim candlelight in a darkened room.

Clear quartz crystal can be used in sunlight, in moonlight, or by candlelight.

Sparkling yellow citrine is wonderful for readings concerning all health matters, conventional healing, and new beginnings, and for questions about learning, travel, house moves, justice, speculation and risks of all kind, and career. It is also good for Spirit Guide work and for receiving and absorbing energy. Citrine will attract prosperity to your home, especially if your work is based there. Citrine is best read in sunlight or clear daylight.

Amethyst is a very gentle scrying tool, good for answering questions about healing, especially alternative methods, and for sending healing. Scryers use it for inducing and interpreting clairvoyant dreams, for matters concerning the past, for complex relationships such as love affairs or step-families, for issues concerning women, and for issues of guilt and blame, spiritual matters, private worries, fears, and addictions. Amethyst is best in moonlight or candlelight.

Smoky quartz is a good medium for past life recall while looking into its depths, and for communicating with ghostly presences, as it is naturally protective. It is also good for all questions concerning endings and loss, for worries about older people, finding items, animals, and people that are lost or missing, issues of attack and protection, and for looking into the distant future. Smoky quartz is surprisingly good in sunlight when held up to the light or in candlelight.

Rose quartz is a naturally healing crystal and good for understanding past or present abuse or unkindness, and for all questions about love, family, animals, fertility, self esteem, the home, and children. Some rose quartz can be quite translucent (shining and reflecting its inner light from the surface) and you would use this for surface shadow scrying (see Chapter 14). It is good in moonlight or soft natural light but not bright sunlight and it is not so effective with candles.

Traditional Preparatory Rituals for Crystal Ball Scrying

There are many medieval versions of cleansing and preparatory rituals for crystal sphere work, though the original creators' names have often been lost. They involved calling on the holy names of God from the Hebrew tradition, or invoking seven or nine Archangels. Because religion and magic were very closely linked, Elizabethan astrologer Sir John Dee would pray in Latin before his assistant, the infamous Edward Kelley, began scrying, and afterward would close the elaborate rite "in the name of the Father, Son and Holy Spirit."

An approximate translation of one of his preliminary prayers is: "Oh Lord most High, send your Light and your Truth to lead us to your Holy Mountain and to the tabernacle of heaven." Perfumes and incenses were used and complex magical seals drawn to prepare the area for scrying.

If you want to read more of these older religious magical practices based on the belief that angels, spirits, and even demons could be commanded within the glass, I would recommend reading works such as the _Three Books of Occult Philosophy_ by 16th-century occultist Heinrich Cornelius Agrippa or Sir John Dee's _Enochian Magick_. (See the Useful Reading section.) They are also available widely online.

I would advise you use caution, however magical these chants sound, usually written in Hebrew or Latin, in summoning spirits with unfamiliar names to aid your scrying or drawing signs you do not fully understand. In those times, even monks might dabble perilously close to the borders of black magic.

I think it is important to find ways of working with the crystal ball that maintain the connection with the spiritual world but fit in with our own 21st-century lives and make personal sense. You can cleanse and dedicate a crystal sphere in the same way I described for clear mirrors.

The Blessings of Raziel

The following angelic dedication, calling upon Raziel, the Archangel of magic and divination the hidden world, is safe and does induce the gentle sense of higher awareness that is an integral part of crystal sphere scrying.

Raziel is credited with writing the esoteric Book of the Angel Raziel that contained all earthly and heavenly knowledge. He gave it to Adam as consolation for losing Eden, but other angels became jealous and threw it into the sea.

Dedicating Your Crystal Ball to Raziel

The first dedication of the ball should be around twilight or just before dawn. Saturday is a good day for your dedication.

Just after dusk or before dawn, the times of Raziel, light a dark green candle (Raziel's color) and from it a pine, myrrh, or poppy (opium) incense stick. Set the crystal ball in front of the candle.

Before you begin the dedication, cleanse your ball with a hyssop or pennyroyal infusion that you have made in advance. Hyssop has been used in religion and magic for thousands of years for purification. Hyssop is best used dried (any of the aerial parts), and you can buy it already powdered.

In silence, sprinkle the ball with a few drops of cooled infusion and then dry and polish it with a cloth made of a soft, natural fabric. Ask as you sprinkle the water in your mind that the sphere is cleansed of all that is not beautiful and sacred.

Then, as you polish the ball, a simple but effective way to empower it, you can ask that it be filled with goodness and light.

Then in silence, taking the incense stick in the hand you write with, write your name in the incense smoke over the ball to make your own.

Then draw Solomon's Seal in smoke over the ball to fill the ball with wisdom. Solomon's Seal is a very old and very positive mystical symbol that unites different spiritual paths. It is based on the sacred triangle. The triangle represents the number three, which is associated with many religions and cultures.

Air   Earth

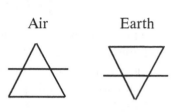

The two triangles of the Seal are the alchemical triangle of the Water Element descending and the triangle of Fire ascending. With the mingling of these Elements, the alchemical triangles of Air and Earth are formed in the Seal.

The triangles of the four Elements—Earth, Air, Fire, and Water—fuse into the middle quintessential shape of five, and the six external points give the magical seven spaces (seven being a sacred number of perfection).

The Triangle of Water

The Triangle of Fire

Solomon's Seal

Ask in silence as you draw the Seal that you may be given the wisdom to use your crystal ball for the good of others, and to discover follow your true path. Next, pass the ball three times around the candle flame clockwise, again asking in silence that your may see visions of truth within its depths and interpret its secrets wisely.

Finally, breathe on the ball three times very softly and slowly and then say aloud, "Raziel, you who know all secrets and all mysteries, reveal to me in this crystal what I most need to know and give me the power to use that knowledge wisely and for the good of all."

Breathe softly three more times. The crystal is now ready for use. You can dedicate other crystal spheres in the same way as you acquire them.

Generally, you will just sprinkle your crystal ball with infusion or still mineral water if you do not have any infusion to cleanse it, and then polish it to empower the ball. However, you can repeat the dedication whenever there is an important occasion. Otherwise, do it monthly.

Attuning to Its Energies

Now that the crystal is yours, you can enjoy getting to know it at your own pace. Crystal scrying is a multi-sensory experience.

Raise your crystal ball cupped gently in both hands, towards the sun, moon, or candlelight, according to the kind of crystal so the light is reflected within it, but does not obscure it.

Holding a crystal is the way to get in touch with it through the psychometric powers of psychic touch you have in the sensitive palms of your hands and fingertips. Look through half-closed eyes at the patterns of flickering light on and within the reflective surface so that you become attuned to its energies. Each crystal sphere is unique and has a guardian whose energies you will sense as you hold it towards the light.

For some scryers, this guardian reveals a distinct personality almost immediately and, if you open your eyes wide and look into the crystalline depth, you may see him or her quite clearly in the crystal. You can use this attunement with the guardian each time you begin scrying after you have cleansed and empowered your ball. Even the smallest spheres possess a benign spirit who is part of the crystal.

Before you begin scrying, ask the help of the guardian that you may see clearly and, if working for others, speak the truth kindly and always with the purpose of showing possibilities and bringing hope and healing.

Beginning Crystal Ball Scrying

When outdoors, work near fragrant flowers or greenery. When indoors, burn a ceremonial fragrance, such as frankincense, sandalwood, one of the Raziel incenses, or a floral scent either as an incense stick or an oil burner fragrance. If you prefer, have a dish of scented potpourri or flowers on the table, as fragrance heightens the psychic senses.

If you use a single candle, you can create a sphere of light within the ball to lead you into it, though you do not want to see the actual candle reflected in the sphere.

If you are reading for more than one person, polish the ball in between sessions and then blow on it three times softly to clear the energies of the previous reading.

Some scryers place the ball on a dark cloth, a special stand, or a dark surface while reading. Because I suggest holding the ball all the time or passing it to the client to establish tactile contact, the dark cloth is not so essential unless you like the idea.

Seeing and Interpreting Images

To begin scrying, hold the ball so the light from whatever source sparkles within and animates the inside of the ball. Reading a sphere with inclusions is almost instant, and the physical eye will reveal images that hold the psychic information you need.

Some expert crystal ball readers always *see* the images in their mind's eye with great clairvoyant accuracy. However, the vast majority can read a crystal ball almost spontaneously. It is just a question of believing whether you can do it or not.

Turn the ball around in your hands as you study the crystalline world within it and enjoy the experience.

Relax and allow pictures to form within the ball one after the other, at first without trying to analyze them, using the cracks and lines within to form animals, birds, stars, scenes, and people.

Though the images are small, they are usually very clear and detailed if you study them, and they don't fade out of view the way mirror or water images do. For example, the woman you see may be carrying flowers or holding her arms and feet similar to a dancer. Get as much visual information as you can from each image. The images are usually three-dimensional.

When you feel confident, focus on one image you see clearly and add aloud what you feel about it and how it relates to your life. Does it answer any questions or explain something that was puzzling you? Record the session on cassette if you wish, or have a pen and paper to scribble images and brief notes as you go along.

Images may, after you have studied them for a while, change into others, a sure sign they are closely related in meaning. Though images are often symbolic, you may see a sudden clear picture of an actual scene. People you can identify specifically, whether a deceased grandmother or a friend who lives across the world, will bring a special message into your mind if you pause and listen.

The next stage is to ask a specific question and allow the images you see to build up clues to the answer.

Initials within the sphere refer to people you know. If you see a number of letters in the ball, write them down and they will form or almost form whole words when rearranged. If initials are unfamiliar, note them and within a week the person will usually have come into your life.

Numbers have significance according to the preset time frame of the question which you should establish before a reading in weeks, months, or more rarely years unless you are working for a long-term prediction.

If you really can't see anything in the ball, it may be because your physical and analytical senses are much slower than your psychic senses to process the information. Stare intensely into the center of the ball until your eyes want to close.

Close your eyes slowly, open them slowly, blink, look into the ball again, and name aloud what you think or sense you *see*. This is invariably accurate.

Afterward, if you look more slowly into the ball you may be able to identify the actual image you sensed, now made up of the cracks and lines. Even if you can't, say what you feel about the image you sensed. The trick is to be really fast before logic tells you it's a load of rubbish. This method can be used quite freely to identify and analyze any number of images. Weave them into a sequence or even a story, and then move on to scrying for what happens next.

Reading for Others

The ball is probably the most interactive way of answering questions for others, whether they be friends, family members, or clients, because you can answer their questions by tapping into their unique image system. It is ideal for unblocking someone who is very anxious. These clients may seem initially unresponsive or hostile even to a reading they have requested (guaranteed to block your natural intuitive flow).

Before asking for a specific question or about any particular issues they want to consider, allow them to hold your crystal ball, look into it, and identify any pictures they see.

Explain that they can use the cracks to make an outline and suggest a whole lot of things people commonly see, such as stars, birds, animals, houses, figures, and landscapes, and say that these usually symbolize an event, relationship, or situation in the scryer's life.

Usually you get instant excited responses from the other person and you can build on this enthusiasm to lead into specific issues quite naturally.

Otherwise, you can ask for any specific questions and time frames at an appropriate moment early in the scrying session. Some people genuinely just want to know what appears. This open-ended approach will often narrow down to background issues under question (there are always some even if unspoken) from the images that appear during the session.

If they are uncertain about seeing images, point out a fairly obvious image you can see (of course, these change every time you use the ball)—"There is the head of the horse, there are its legs. Can you see it galloping?"—so that they know the kind of pictures they are looking for.

Of course they may disagree and say, *"No, it is a unicorn because it has a horn on its head."* At that point, you are instantly plugged into their inner imaging system. The interflow of energies as you pass the ball between you is excellent for clairvoyance, and you can cleanse your ball afterward.

Ask if any words came into their mind when they saw an image and what they feel about the image. For example, if they saw a bird, what sort of a bird was it? Was it flying bird, a nesting bird, a bird of prey, or a caged bird? What species of bird is it? Is it one they like or fear? Is the cage door open, and, if so, does the bird want to stay inside?

Then take the ball in your own hands and try to locate the same image and describe your impressions. Hand the ball back and ask them to identify another image and then a third. Encourage as much detail as possible, and with each image try to locate it yourself and add your impressions.

When they have identified as many images as they can, look into the ball yourself and describe in detail any new images you see. If they do not want to look for images at all, you can lead the whole process. But in this case ask after each image what it means to them. You do often hone in on a really relevant symbol that can hold the key to what is troubling them.

Afterward, you can put all the information together and steer the conclusion-making process so that they reach their own conclusions. I believe the mark of a gifted clairvoyant is to get your clients or people you are working with to answer their own questions with your help. That way you are not interfering with their destiny.

For example, the bird sitting inside the cage that is open may be too scared to fly out, may not want to, or may not realize the door is open. Who is the bird (usually the person who has asked for the reading)?

Ask them who the bird signifies, even if it is obvious to you. What is the cage? A relationship, a job going nowhere, a home that has become confined, an illness that is holding them back? How do the other images expand the theme or give new direction? Whether alone or working with someone else you can weave the images together to find a solution.

Structuring a Crystal Reading

If you prefer, you can structure a reading by specifying a number of images you will seek, and what stage each of those images refers to. Three is normal, but you can use more, as long as you assign the meanings in advance.

If working with three, you could designate the first image as representing the issue as it is now, the second as any suggested action or reaction, and the third as the outcome of that potential action. However, be open to any extra images that appear spontaneously, for the structure is only a guideline.

You can also work with a partner or family member with the crystal ball to resolve a joint issue or problem by weaving in the images you each saw and discussing what each of you felt around them.

It is also a creative, non-confrontational way, whether in a more open-minded workplace or in a family, to pass the ball around a circle of people, each person contributing an image to answer a joint question. One person acts as a scribe and everyone joins in the interpretation.

After any reading, thank your guardian of the ball you have been using and say goodbye until you meet again. This cuts the psychic connection with the ball and returns you to the everyday world.

Cleanse your ball as suggested at the beginning of the chapter or using the following methods, and put it away either in a dark cloth or leave it open to empower your scrying place to spread harmony though the home and to attract abundance, health, and happiness.

The 3 Crystals Method to Reveal Past, Present, and Future

This tends to be a very personal method to decide your ongoing path. Other psychic senses are very important, especially clairaudience—words that spontaneously appear in your head as you identify the images.

Recording the session can be helpful. Speak spontaneously aloud in a stream of words so you are not slowed psychically by trying to make sense of it all as you experience each image or impression.

For this you need three different crystal spheres that can be quite small: an amethyst sphere to show you the past that is relevant to the present, clear quartz to show your present, and finally a smoky quartz for the future yet unrevealed. You can substitute rose quartz for amethyst and citrine for smoky quartz if you prefer.

If you don't have three crystal balls then you can use the same one, preferably a clear quartz, but keep to three separate stages and, after each stage, blow on the ball and pass your hands over it three times counterclockwise, palms down, a few inches above the ball.

Set the three balls in a row, left to right, past, present, and future, as you face them. Cleanse and polish each before you begin and ask the help of its individual guardian.

Begin the scrying by closing your eyes as you hold the ball of the past first. Define aloud, "I seek to know whatever from the past will help me in the present and to make the future better." Run your fingertips over the sphere and let thoughts, impressions, words, and images flow. Then, open your eyes and look into the ball, using the inner markings to identify an image.

Finally, close your eyes and, holding the ball, say, "The message from the past is…" and speak the message from the Guardian of the sphere without hesitation. Repeat with the other two balls, changing the words. For the present you would say,

"I seek to know whatever may be unclear in the present that will help me to make the future better" and "The message from the present is...." For the ball of the future you would say, "I seek to know whatever may occur in the future that I may change or shape as I wish." Afterward say, "The message for the future is...."

Cleanse each ball right to left and thank each guardian in turn. When you have time, listen quietly to the recording and you may find that extra insights come.

Regular Cleansing and Empowerment

Crystal Pendulum

Hold a crystal pendulum up to the light, whether sun, moon, or candleligh,t and twirl it freely so it spins. Pass it counterclockwise nine times about 2 inches above the ball, to cleanse it. If you use this method at the beginning of a session to empower the ball after cleansing, turn it nine times clockwise above the ball.

If following cleansing by empowerment, plunge the pendulum nine times into a glass of clear water after the counterclockwise movements and hold it up to the light again.

Empowered Sun, Moon, or Amethyst Water

For cleansing and empowering clear quartz, citrine, or smoky quartz ball, leave a small bowl of water covered with fine mesh from dawn until noon to fill it with sunlight. This will work even if the sun is not shining, and you can put the water out before bedtime if dawn is very early. You can store some in a clear glass bottle in your fridge for up to three weeks.

For an amethyst or rose quartz ball (also for selenite; see Chapter 14), leave water out all night on the night of the full moon from sunset when it rises and then bottle the water in a dark glass bottle. You can make this in advance and store it in your fridge until the next full moon.

For any ball cleansing and empowerment, soak an amethyst overnight in clear water indoors or out, take out the amethyst, and use the water for cleansing or empowering any scrying tools. Make this fresh the night before and throw away any left over on to soil.

Sprinkle the water over the ball to cleanse it, and then polish it to empower it. If putting it away/finishing the session, you can leave the ball to dry naturally rather than polishing it.

Breath and Light

Use candlelight, silver for amethyst and rose quartz and gold for clear quartz, citrine or smoky quartz or moonlight (waxing and full only) or sunlight respectively.

Breathe in the light slowly and gently, picturing it slowly filling your body with silver or gold light. On the out breath *see* dark light flowing from you similar to mist. When you feel filled with light, blow very softly on the ball three times as you hold it in your hands to cleanse it and three times to empower it, picturing the light flowing and around the ball so it glows softly.

If cleansing alone after a session, hold the ball and let the energies of light flow between you, picturing them getting paler and softer until there is just gentle soothing white light.

This is a wonderful personal self-empowering ritual, holding the ball at any time you feel anxious, hyped, or afraid.

Incense or Smudge

Use a mini-smudge in sagebrush, cedar, or best of all for crystal balls, sweetgrass, lavender, or rose incense stick. Swirl counterclockwise three times to cleanse and three times clockwise to empower.

With smudge/incense, even if you are cleansing the crystal sphere at the end of a session, begin by facing the four main compass directions in turn, holding the lighted smudge stick directly ahead at a 60-degree angle, starting in the North.

Then, facing North again (you can use approximations for the directions), raise the stick upwards to honor Father Sky and then down to honor Mother Earth and swirl it around yourself in spirals as the seventh direction. Leave the smudge to burn out.

Using Salt

Some practitioners pack a new ball in a container of salt, but I do worry about the physical effects on the crystal.

If you prefer, you can sprinkle a counterclockwise circle of salt enclosing the crystal to cleanse, an outer ring clockwise to empower, and then, when you are cleansing it after, use just a final counterclockwise circle.

After the session, scoop up the salt and dispose of it under running water.

Hyssop or Pennyroyal

Use as crystal water (also see the chapter on infusions).

Clouds and Colors

Some scryers see colored clouds in a clear mirror or crystal ball instead of images. This may be a transitional phase especially in mirror work, as a prelude to seeing colored images.

But other competent clairvoyants always see colored clouds rather than actual images and interpret these through inner images in their mind and their clairaudient system. This is not a system you can learn, and many clairvoyants do not ever experience it.

- Ascending clouds indicate a positive outcome, recognition, increased finances, and improvements.

- Descending clouds suggest delays, cancellations, temporary losses, or cash flow problems.

- Clouds moving to the right indicate helpful influences; those moving to the left suggest that you should beware of opposition.

- White clouds imply a positive decision or answer, good health, and the favorable outcome of any issue under question.

- Black clouds suggest a negative response and advise caution in any projected undertakings until things improve.

- If the dark clouds suddenly become lighter, wait for the right moment that will bring success or happiness.

- If light clouds gets darker there may be tantrums, quarrels, and frustration.

- Light shades of any color are a good omen; darker shades are less auspicious.

- Green clouds talk of happiness in love and also of future good fortune.

- Blue clouds promise success in a money or career matter or that justice will be served, and also house moves and the successful resolution of official matters

- Violet clouds herald helpful friends, secrets revealed, and what is lost, returned, or found.

≈ Pink clouds indicate someone new coming into your life, or a new beginning, family harmony, and reconciliation.

≈ Brown clouds talk of domestic and practical matters, the stabilizing of finances, and settling down in home or home improvements. They're also auspicious for property matters.

≈ Silver clouds promise consolation and healing, but definitely a change for the better, and are good for matters concerning fertility and motherhood.

≈ Gold clouds mean dreams coming true and ambitions fulfilled, and fathers and fatherhood.

≈ Red clouds warn of anger, strong emotions but also self-initiated changes, passion, and the lifting of stagnation.

≈ Orange clouds indicate creativity, self-confidence, independence, and self-employment.

≈ Yellow clouds signify success in learning, tests, success in speculation, gambling, and risk-taking. They also represent malice, envy, and jealousy.

Chapter 13

Scrying With Tea Leaves and Coffee Grounds

The most homely form of scrying is examining tea or coffee grounds found at the side or in the bottom of a cup after drinking the hot liquid. Reading tea leaves and coffee grounds is called Tasseography, or Tasseomancy.

It needs no cleansing of tools apart from almost-boiling water, customarily added to warm the tea or coffee pot before making the beverage. Though we may think of Romany tea cup fortune tellers or bejeweled practitioners in the dark corners of 18th-century European coffeehouses, the majority of tea and coffee divinations take place around the kitchen table or with cups of cappuccino in a corner of the office.

There are gifted male scryers; however, it is thought of mainly as a woman's art. The family matriarch would use the markings left in the tea or coffee cup to dispense good advice, based on what her intuitive senses derived from the shapes and patterns. The secrets of interpretation were usually handed down through the female line, but the art might also be learned by watching the elders reading the cups.

The History of Tea and Tea Leaf Reading

In Chinese tradition, tea was used in China as early as 3000 B.C.E. as one of the elixirs of long life. Tea, it was said, came out of the cosmic egg when the Divine Artisan was creating the world. According to Buddhist legend the first tea leaves fell from the eyelids of the meditating Holy One, who cut them off to prevent himself from falling asleep while he was meditating.

In ancient China, monks ceremonially drank milkless tea in bell-shaped cups without handles, and derived wisdom from reading the leaves left in the bottom.

Tea was used for divination in the Orient from almost the beginning, and the tea ceremonies still practiced in Japan today have their roots in early meditation and creating a quiet space in which insight can come spontaneously. From China, the secrets of its cultivation and divination spread to India and Sri Lanka, the former Ceylon. From India, the Romany gypsies brought the magical art to Europe.

Tea did not arrive in England much before the middle of the 17th century and was very expensive, costing from $10 to $20 per pound sterling, in the prices of that period. It traveled to America with the early colonists, where it shared popularity with coffee until the infamous Boston Tea Party in 1773 made tea-drinking unpatriotic and the English became the bad guys.

It was not until 1885 that tea from India and Ceylon (now Sri Lanka) reached England in any quantity, and so even in Victorian times tea was a great luxury, kept in a locked wooden box by the lady of the house.

But the art of divination from the dregs left behind in a cup or glass was practiced in Europe much earlier. Wine dregs were consulted, a craft known as oinomancy. From early times, too, peasant women made herbal brews for minor ailments and to preserve good health. Afterward, leaves from the brews would be used by the family matriarch to discover the root cause of the distress.

Tasseography has remained primarily the art of the Romany gypsy or of the home rather than the professional clairvoyant.

Areas of the Cup

There are agreed traditional meanings according to where tea leaves are sited in the cup. It may be that this method of reading does not suit you and you prefer, as with any other form of scrying, to weave the images wherever they appear into a coherent whole and be purely image led.

Decide in advance whether or not you are considering cup positions and your psyche will provide the information within the parameters you set.

I prefer to interpret the image meaning regardless of where they appear in the cup. Even if you do apply assigned meanings, allow the image to speak to you and to explain the connection.

You can divide the inside of the cup into vertical imaginary quarters around the circumference to tell you to what the image is referring to, and then three horizontal bands moving downwards that pass through the quadrants to suggest a possible time frame.

The Quadrants

The quadrants extend vertically through the top to bottom of the cup.

1: The area round the handle inside the cup furthest from you

The area around the handle of the cup as you look towards it represents events or people close to you, such as family or close friends and your home. The area close to or touching the handle on either side of it, signifies the present life of the scryer. These tend to indicate emotional events or interactions rather than movement.

2: The opposite side of the cup from the handle, nearest to you

This is the realm of strangers, acquaintances, colleagues, and matters away from the home, including work and travel. These can talk about your reactions, interactions, and personal goals rather than movement, which is dealt with in the next two quadrants. A crowd here can suggest either that this is the most dominant area of life currently, or that there are concerns with the outer world. It can also refer to places not yet visited that will be important.

3: The quadrant to the left of the handle (beyond the handle quadrant joining area 2)

Images here represent people and events from the past who still play, or may return to play, a role, or people moving out of the questioner's life. Any large or very dark images here can suggest that there may be unresolved matters from the past that are affecting the current issue, especially if this area is crowded.

4: The quadrant to the right of the handle (completing the circle)

Symbols here are indicative of people and events moving into your life. You may find these images more shadowy and incomplete, suggesting that present actions are making one particular set of events more likely than another.

If this area is blank, it does not mean there is no future, but that energies are concentrated on present or even past endeavours.

Time Frames

These are the horizontal bands moving down the cup.

The Top Third

Traditional interpretations suggest events or people represented by leaves near the rim of the cup as occurring or changing their influence in the near future, within weeks or even days. You can learn more from the quadrant positions.

So if you get an image in the quadrant to the left of the handle high up in the cup, it suggests someone from the past who still exerts an influence over you will suddenly move out of your life or have less power over you. The closer to the top, the sooner it will occur.

The Middle Segment of the Cup

Leaves halfway down the cup suggest significant events or changes within a few months (again according to which quadrant they appear in).

The Bottom Third of the Cup

The area close to the bottom of the cup is believed to portray the more distant future, maybe even a year or even more.

If you do get a contradictory message (for example an image at the bottom of the cup in the quadrant of the past), this might indicate that past events will still be influencing you years from now—unless you decided to put them behind you or break free. Be creative in fitting the interpretations together.

Good vs. Bad Omens

I ignore the good vs. bad omens, but some tea leaf readers count the number of each to see if there are more positive than negative factors about the question overall. It can also clash with the timings interpretation, unless you study stray random leaves or clumps and piles of leaves that do not make or form part of an image.

Leaves near the top of the cup may indicate that there are no obstacles to be overcome in a particular issue, or that present circumstances promise happiness.

Tea leaves from the center upwards indicate that, apart from a few minor details, any current aims should be attained or that life in general will be peaceful for a while.

Leaves in the lower half of the cup suggest that there may be some challenges and obstacles to overcome to achieve any goal, but that persistence will pay off.

The bottom of the cup, with both stray leaves and actual images, was regarded in the old methods as foretelling tears and sorrow. More positively, leaves or images here indicate that it may be necessary to compromise to succeed and that setbacks can be turned to your advantage with patience.

A pile of leaves at the side of the cup opposite from the handle suggests that obstacles need the cooperation of others to overcome them; a pile of leaves close to the handle says that the solution lies in your hands or independent action.

Symbols in Tea Leaf Reading

These may vary considerably. The largest symbol is usually the dominant one. If the symbol is large in relation to the others, then it may represent, according to the meaning of the symbol, a large success or sum of money or a major problem.

If a symbol is clear and well-formed, then the issue is clear-cut or the offer or relationship is definite. Mistiness and unfinished outlines suggest that all may not be as clear as it seems. It might also indicate that a problem appears larger than it really is because of personal fears.

The Alphabet

Letters of the alphabet, usually in pairs, appear in the tea leaves and coffee grounds far more than in other kinds of scrying.

They represent important people in your life or the name of someone new, whether a helpful stranger, a new friend, lover, or business acquaintance, according to the quadrant. You will be able to discover the identity, depending on where the image appears in the cup and/or what you feel intuitively.

The position of the letter is indicative of the relationship: the closer to the handle, the closer the relationship either emotionally or location-wise. If the letter is very near the handle, then the meeting will occur close to home, involve home events, or be love-related.

Numbers

Numbers tend to represent the number of units of time that will elapse before an event occurs. The time scale is taken from the horizontal band of the cup in which the number appears.

For example, a number 8 right at the top of the cup might indicate eight days, in the top third eight weeks, below the center eight months, and at the bottom of the cup eight years.

This time scale is applied to the symbol to which it is closest— that is, a 6 next to a boat or plane below the center of the cup might suggest an unexpected and significant journey overseas in about six months (close to the handle and it might be a romance that becomes true love). However, some people do not like to try and forecast time so accurately, preferring a general indication of possibilities.

If a number occurs in isolation, it can be interpreted independently with the following meanings.

- 1 indicates a new beginning, energy, and decision, and says that any action, taken whether in connection with a relationship or work, or starting a new venture, promises well.

- 2 suggests that relationships are the predominant issue whether love, family, or at work, and that you may need to balance the demands of different people or aspects of your life.

∽ **3** is the number of expansion, perhaps an addition to your family or circle of friends. It can as easily be a new step-relation rather than a baby. Alternatively, it may represent new responsibility that could lead to future prosperity or satisfaction.

∽ **4** is the number of feeling restricted and frustrated but suggests that a slow, methodical path may be the best in the long run and that it is not a time for risks or short-cuts, whether in money or relationships.

∽ **5** in tea leaf reading suggests restlessness and a desire for change in a particular aspect of life. It suggests that a change of approach or perspective may be better than giving up.

∽ **6** talks of harmony and reconciliation, of recognizing your own worth and achievement, and of developing links with others socially or at work.

∽ **7** is a very magical number, indicating the unexpected and exciting. Rely on your intuition and take a chance if one is offered.

∽ **8** is the number of widening your horizons, perhaps moving on to another phase in your life, taking a risk, and not worrying about past mistakes.

∽ **9** is the number of achievement in a personal way, the desire for perfection, ambition, and independence or self-employment.

Shapes

Circles

Circles or rings are often regarded as the most fortunate of shapes, indicating happiness or success. If the circle is interpreted as a ring, it may suggest a permanent commitment of the heart, even marriage. Although some tea leaf readers say only a thick circle should be regarded as a ring, it really is an individual interpretation.

If accompanied by a bell, another traditional wedding symbol, the ring would suggest an imminent attachment, especially if near the top of the cup.

A broken circle or ring never foretells the end of a relationship or happiness. Rather, it says that the questioner may be worried about a broken relationship or one that seems to be floundering. However, with good will it can perhaps be resolved, especially if the break is only partial in the circle. The surrounding symbols can offer advice as to the problem and, most importantly, how it can be best mended.

Crosses

A cross can indicate burdens, either imposed by others or just a general feeling of being weighed down by the demands of life. Traditional lore gets very gloomy about a cross within a circle, indicating confinement in a hospital or even prison.

However, the restrictions are usually those of a situation in everyday life or connected with justice or officialdom that cannot at present be changed. This can mean that needless energy is wasted fretting instead of planning for when movement is possible, or finding something good about each day.

A cross inside a square suggests that the questioner is making barriers, perhaps because he or she does not want change.

Squares

Squares represent protection rather than restriction. However, if a person is being too protective, then the situation may feel stifling, and it is time to try to push back the boundaries of personal freedom. Often, the square appears close to a symbol of a house, which may suggest that material security.

Stalks

Stalks traditionally indicate people and may appear with an initial. Often an accompanying symbol gives a clue to the identity. If not, let your intuition guide you. The stalk will be someone who is prominent in your life at present, either because of a developing relationship or perhaps a problem in dealings with this person.

Two or three stalks together can suggest a family, or that there is a choice or conflict of loyalties. Let your intuition guide you. If a stalk is straight, then the person is reliable; if it is wavy, he or she may waver according to circumstance.

Dots

Dots in groups indicate money, usually money coming in, perhaps from an unexpected source or a project bearing fruit. The number can suggest whether the windfall is likely to be small or large. Small single dots often refer to correspondence, perhaps a job offer, contract, or news that may lead to money-making opportunities. A single large dot may be a gift or payment in kind. Some people count small dots as months and long ones as years.

Lines

Lines talk of journeys; the length of the line suggests whether the journey is close or further away. Clear, straight lines suggest easy journeys; broken ones indicate that any planned travel arrangements should be double-checked, and if possible allowing plenty of time and an alternative means of transport or back-up route.

On a less-practical level, lines can refer to any kind of venture and, if straight, promise a direct route to success or happiness.

Dashes or Broken Lines

Dashes mean that journey plans may be delayed or interrupted, or that an enterprise that needs ingenuity and perseverance will not be quickly realized.

Rectangles

A rectangle can indicate that disagreements or unfair criticism can hinder progress, whether at work or in a relationship. Usually, this is due to rigid attitudes on the part of others and so it is important to avoid potential areas of conflict where possible.

Triangles

Triangles are a magical shape and so indicate success and unexpected possibilities, as well as pregnancy and additions to the family. However, if the apex of the triangle is pointing towards the bottom of the cup or away from the handle, then opportunities are in danger of being missed unless swift action is taken.

Tea Leaf Readings

Tea leaf reading is a good group activity among friends or family where you can sit around answering one another's questions. The slow, easy atmosphere begins with making the tea, perhaps using crockery that has been in the family for generations. It grows while drinking slowly and chatting over concerns. Finally, the almost-ritualistic reading of the leaves, following rules unchanged for centuries, makes this a perfect scrying tool for anyone. The following method comes from my family tradition and is quite a common one. However, if it does not feel right for you, devise your own that seems more natural.

Use firm, separate leaves of a traditional brew such as Earl Grey or Darjeeling. Some people like to keep a small canister of tea especially for readings. Warm the teapot with water that has not quite boiled and rinse it out. As you do this, visualize all the conscious worries and blocks disappearing. This counts as cleansing.

Put a spoonful of tea in the pot for each person, plus one for the pot. Let the rest of the water reach boiling point, add it to the pot, and leave for three to four minutes, unstirred, and longer for a stronger brew. In industrial areas of Britain, the Brown Betty is the traditional teapot used for tea leaf reading, which is a plain, dark brown pot. If you can acquire one, they are best for use in tea leaf readings.

Use a large, shallow cup, plain on the inside. A clear glass, heat-resistant cup is also very effective, as you can see your reading from both sides. Don't buy one of the special fortune-telling cups, as they are marked in ways that will actually inhibit your natural scrying abilities.

Fill the cup with tea, and most of the leaves will sink to the bottom. Do not strain the tea or use tea bags. Add milk and sugar or lemon.

Even when you cup is full you can derive meanings.

- A single tea leaf floating on the surface of the cup of tea heralds unexpected money coming to the questioner.

- Several leaves floating indicate happy days ahead.

- A clear surface promises rest and relaxation, even an unexpected holiday.

- A single leaf stuck to the side of a cup of tea above the level of liquid suggests meeting a new friend, or romance for the unattached.

Drink the tea and, if alone, plan the questions you will ask, or talk them over with a friend. Absolutely any question can be asked, but family, love, home, health, good luck, money worries, children, and animal subjects seem to be very effective.

Preparing the Cup

After drinking, leave just enough liquid in the bottom of the cup so that the leaves are still floating.

The traditional method for tea leaf reading is to swirl the remaining tea around in the cup in a counterclockwise direction three times with the opposite hand from the one you write with.

Place the inverted cup on the saucer to drain the remaining liquid by turning the inverted cup another three times in a counterclockwise direction while on the saucer, once again using the opposite hand. Men can, according to custom, turn the cup clockwise on each occasion. A wide saucer is best.

Leave it for a minute to drain away. Turn the cup right side up and begin reading the leaves stuck to the sides and bottom of the cup, with the handle furthest away from you. Cradle the cup in your hand for the psychometric fingertip connection.

Twist and turn the cup if you need to, but calculate the position of the images in the cup with the handle facing toward you. You can drain and turn the cup a different way if this method feels unnatural.

Reading the Leaves

Peer into the cup until you can see distinct images in the leaves. Traditionally, leaves are read from the top of the cup in a clockwise direction downward, left to right. However, you can look at the whole cup first for an overview, or, if there is one particularly clear image in the cup, you may wish to start with that. Notice the area of the cup in which it appears. The images formed are similar to children's stick men or outline drawings.

Refloat the leaves in a little boiling water and drain them again if you can make no sense of the images (very unusual).

The tea leaves are a focus or trigger for pictures from deep within your mind and so it may be that a group of leaves suggests a scene or detailed picture. The best tea leaf readers are ones who trust intuition and inspiration, and see with the clairvoyant mind's eye as well as the physical one.

It is at all not unlucky to read your own tea leaves (a superstition without foundation). If you are working alone, use pen and paper to scribble down representations of the images one by one and any words that come to mind. Tea leaf reading is a stream-of-consciousness method, and you may find that a whole stream of seemingly unrelated ideas flows from a single image.

Put the cup on the table where you can see the image and then write, transferring your gaze between the image and the paper, or better still focusing in the cup, as you write.

Do not stop to read what you wrote, but end with a drawn representation of the image to remind you, and note which part of the cup the image was in (upper left near the handle, right in the bottom in the center). Each position has a traditional meaning.

Then pick up the cup again (the psychometric fingertip connection is very important) and again look into the cup for the next image, left to right, moving down. When you have finished, read what you have written and a coherent answer to your question will have been created, together with suggestions for action or cautions to patience.

If reading for others in a group, one person asks the question, swirls, and inverts his or her own cup, identifies an image, says what it seems to be, but does not go into detail. He or she then passes the cup to the next person who identifies another image in it, says what it looks like in relation to the question, and so on. One person can act as scribe and write down the image names.

Then when no more pictures are identifiable, the image names are read out and discussed individually, then pieced together to answer the question. The second person then asks a question, and his or her cup is studied by all present.

If you have plenty of time or there are just two or three of you, the first person whose question the reading is answering, having identified his or her first image, shows it to the person on the right, who may see it differently. That second interpretation is added, and the second scryer shows the image to the person on the right.

When everyone has interpreted the first picture in the cup, a second image is identified by the person whose question it is, he or she shows it to the next person, and so on.

This is another good method with a nervous client, especially on a first visit. Ask the person for whom you are reading what the main question or issue is.

Pick out the first image to demonstrate the kind of pictures that can be seen in the cup and show your client how you make up the picture from the leaves or grains. Give her the cup and ask her what she feels about the image you saw. Ask her to identify another image and what it seems to be saying. Encourage the questioner to guide the reading and draw their own conclusions.

Coffee Ground Reading

Coffee drinking and readings came from the Arabian world, where coffee beans were first discovered around 600 C.E.

Legend tell of how the Archangel Gabriel brought a dish of concentrated coffee to revive the dying prophet Mohammed, and so coffee became very special and was kept secret from the Westernized world for centuries.

It was not until the 1700s that coffee became popular in Western Europe and the Americas. However, it is believed that Captain John Smith, who helped to found the colony of Virginia at Jamestown, may have first introduced coffee to North America much earlier in 1607.

Coffee replaced tea as America's beverage after the Boston Tea Party on December 16, 1773. Furious Boston residents threw 342 crates of tea from three ships as a protest against the extortionate tea tax (among other extortionate taxes) imposed by England at the time.

Easy Coffee Ground Reading

You can read coffee grounds for any purpose; they are excellent for career, travel ventures, and creativity, as well as domestic and relationship concerns.

Without realizing it you may already be a coffee ground reader. If you are a regular cappuccino drinker, you may occasionally sit staring into the residue when you have almost emptied the cup.

As you gaze into the almost-empty cup, you may half-consciously have noticed pictures. These interpreted intuitively will open your mind to a wider range of possibilities and information that is not accessible through more conventional means. It works as well with espresso residue at the local Starbucks or brewed coffee in the finest china.

Some practitioners have said if tea leaf reading is the scrying of house and home, coffee ground reading is the crystal ball of the workplace. However, you can just as easily make coffee at home and share an intimate session or get down to some serious private scrying.

Other fast methods for coffee scrying include:

- Add a small spoonfull of coarse ground roast coffee to the liquid left in the percolator or filter machine while it is still warm and stir. (Instant coffee will dissolve so is not so suitable.)

- Scoop up a small spoon of the damp but not too soggy residual coffee grounds from the bottom of whatever method you are using.

- Scatter these grounds on a white plate or flat white dish and blow the grains on the dish while tilting it to create symbols and patterns. If the grounds are too sticky, microwave them for a few seconds on the plate.

- Half-closing your eyes, ask a question and allow the grains to form either a scene or separate images against the white background.

- If you relax you will instinctively interpret the significance of the symbol in the light of your question.

- Spanish/Mexican metal coffee makers, with separate compartments for coffee and water, make good instant divinatory coffee ground collectors after the coffee has been poured (and can be adapted for making Turkish or Middle Eastern coffee).

Making Ground Coffee for Divination

For a simple private reading, you can add a small spoon of ground coffee to a cup, add boiling or near-boiling water, stir well, and leave until the grounds settle in the bottom and drink. It is not the world's greatest cup of coffee, but is just about drinkable and excellent for divination.

If you add milk to the cup soon after the water and stir it, you will get grounds forming images on top as they settle. These moving images will often create a scene that can reveal information about the context of the issue you did not know.

For more than one person, measure ground coffee into a heat-proof coffee pot or jug—1 tablespoon of rough ground coffee to 6 fluid oz. of cold water. Use a measuring jug. Bring the coffee to a boil, then turn down the heat and allow the pot to simmer for a minute. Alternatively, use a vacuum or heat-retaining jug and add boiling water, stirring and putting on the lid.

Do not filter the coffee grounds as you pour the coffee into the cup. Add milk and sugar if you would like it and stir. The grounds will settle on the bottom of the cup.

Once you get near the bottom of the cup and the grounds start to float, invert the cup on a saucer or plate to drain off the liquid. Traditionally, for a woman a cup is turned three times counterclockwise with the receptive hand, the one you do not write with, and clockwise again with the receptive hand for a man. You can turn three more times for luck.

Leave plenty of time for the liquid to drain in the saucer. Turn the cup the right way up. Grains may stick to the sides of the cup as well as the bottom. If any grains transfer to the saucer you can read those, too (see the following pages for interpreting your grounds). Read as you would for tea leaves.

Middle Eastern Traditional Methods

If you are looking for a traditional method, try Middle Eastern coffee readings. The Middle Eastern Bedouin people originally heated their coffee in pots on the hot desert sand.

While I was in Egypt, I learned the art of coffee reading, using the thick, syrupy Middle Eastern coffee. This is slightly different from the conventional coffee grounds method of reading but seems startlingly accurate.

Making Middle Eastern Coffee

You will need a traditional long-handled briki or cezve (you can buy special sets with the pot, small cups, and usually a pack of coffee). Put 2 or 3 teaspoons of sugar for each person in the bottom of the pot.

Some blends you buy have cardamom or figs, or various spices to the coffee and may not need a lot of sugar. Experiment until you get the right brew for you.

Fill the pot with water to where it narrows and fill the rest of the space, up to the rim, with the coffee. Heat over a very low flame until the coffee begins to foam upwards.

Remove from the heat, stir until the foam goes down, put it back on the heat, where it will bubble up again, remove, and stir a second and third time. The coffee is now ready. Stir the coffee well as you pour it into individual cups. The coffee has grounds in it that will sink to the bottom as you pour.

Drink it black. It is already syrupy, so it won't need extra individual sugar.

Egyptian, Greek, or Turkish Coffee Reading

The beauty of this method is that because the coffee is so thick and syrupy, the residue will stick to the sides as well as the bottom.

You can drain off any excess liquid in a saucer by inverting the cup, but what you actually read is, according to my Egyptian source, the white lines and markings of the cup that shows through the dark syrupy residue. The images are very clear and startlingly accurate, in effect a dark canvas though which white lines and shapes shine through.

Initially try this method with coffee in a café that sells Turkish, Greek, or Middle Eastern coffee so you get an idea of the consistency needed.

Some readers drain the cup completely until there is only residue in the bottom, but the method when the residue is still quite damp and coats the inside of the cup is by far the best and most authentic.

Beginning Coffee Reading

Use an ordinary large, shallow white coffee cup for Western coffee. You can read with a white unadorned mug, but the shallower cup makes a reading clearer. Any light-colored cup can be used.

Coffee Ground or Syrup Readings

Coffee images tend to be stronger and firmer than those of tea leaves. In practice you may find that coffee ground readings work better if it is open-ended rather than tied to specific area meanings. The secret of any coffee reading is to half-close your eyes, hold the cup between your cupped hands (rather than by the handle), slowly revolve it clockwise, and, most importantly, keep talking; if alone, scribble notes and pictures between images as you would for tea.

Say what you see without analysis or modification, as this first interpretation is free from conscious blocks that will try to tidy up your thoughts.

Single images may evoke words or impressions in your mind, and this holistic approach is far more helpful than just analyzing the meaning of an individual flower image (though that is a good starting point).

You can either read as many images as there are or choose the first or clearest three and assign them positions. One example is: Image 1—What cannot be changed, Image—2 What can be changed, Image 3—What can be achieved through change. You can assign your own positions to a given number of images. You can, if you want, apply cup positions to this method, but you may end up with inconsistencies of interpretation. For more general readings, read the clearest image first.

With divination of any kind, if you define the area of concern, work, love, or home, then the reading will refer to that. The exception is if a major problem is overshadowing every aspect of your life, such as someone's illness or a breakup, in which case that needs to be dealt with before your psyche can focus happily again on other interactions. You can also interpret a colleague, friend, or family member's coffee grounds, as with tea leaves.

You can, for a joint decision, choose one cup at random from a collected tray of cups after a coffee drinking session, and read that to answer a collective question, passing it around the group to describe images and then all join in to say what they mean.

Alternatively, tip all the dregs from the different cups into a single bowl and either read them as they float, or drain that and pass around the collective drained grounds for general comment.

When I was young, we always had a small bowl in the center of the table so when a cup of tea was finished the dregs were poured into that, leaving the individual cup clear for the inevitable refill.

If lovers or close family members read each other's cups, you may well see similar images in the different cups.

Chapter 14

Scrying With Shadows

Shadow scrying is a very beautiful form of scrying, best carried out in the evening when the world is quieter and our minds are slowing down.

You can scry also in daylight or moonlight with opaque crystals, such as agate eggs or translucent selenite spheres, and with smoke, especially from incense whose fragrance creates an altered and higher state of awareness.

Shadows, whether made by a flickering candle after dark on a light background wall, or cast into pools by trees or clouds, seem to evoke a very gentle awareness of spiritual matters and put the frantic everyday world and worries into perspective

Encountering the Wise Ones

I touched upon the techniques of gazing into dark mirrors for connecting with ancestors and guides. Any form of shadow scrying is very evocative of the presence of wise ancestors, past worlds, and most of all, of Spirit Guides.

Whereas angels shimmer best in clear crystal, the softer light and shadow of a translucent or opaque crystal or incense smoke provides an easy and benign connection with a Spirit Guide so that it seems similar to chatting with an old friend as evening falls.

Angels and Archangels of Twilight and Darkness

Aftiel

Angel of twilight, he is a shadowy angel, best seen outdoors as the last rays of the sun are disappearing, with silvery gray wings and a halo containing the purple of sunset. He is also good for smoke scrying of any kind.

Candle color: Silver gray

Crystal: Silver or rainbow moonstone

Fragrance: Poppy (opium) or lemon verbena

Cassiel

Cassiel is Archangel of the planet Saturn and of Saturday, the angel of compassion, tears, and solitude, who weeps for the sorrows of the world and also helps to heal them. Some have linked him to the primal darkness before creation and also with the twilight hours. Surprisingly he also rules over games of chance and good luck.

He is portrayed as bearded, riding a dragon, and wearing dark robes with indigo flames sparking from his halo.

Good for fire smoke scrying, any dark or opaque crystal, and dark mirrors and connecting with Guides.

Candle color: Indigo/black/dark purple

Fragrance: Patchouli and violet

Crystals: Black tourmaline

Jeduthun

Leading angel of the evening choirs in Heaven. Visualize him with his scrolls of music in the evening light, a faint rainbow formed from the harmony of the notes around his head.

Good for translucent crystal spheres, for oil or water scrying after dusk, and for candles against white walls.

Candle color: Lilac

Crystal: Purple sugilite

Fragrance: Melissa (lemon balm) or thyme

Leliel/Lailah

A female angel of the night, she has deep midnight blue robes and a halo, and her wings are flecked with stars. She will protect the young and vulnerable.

Good for past lives through shadow scrying, ancestor work, incense, and inks at twilight.

Candle color: Dark blue

Crystal: Blue goldstone

Fragrance: Mimosa or jasmine

Scachlil

He is the angel of the sun's dying rays at night and governor of the ninth hour of the day. He flares golden for the last time each night as the sun sinks and wears the colors of a golden twilight.

Good for candle shadow scrying, scrying with smudge sticks, and outdoor smoke scrying of any kind.

Candle color: Burnished or dark gold

Crystal: Polished golden iron pyrites or a brass nugget

Fragrance: Basil or marigold

Deities

Hecate

Ancient Greek Grandmother or Crone goddess of the night and of enchantment; goddess of the crossroads where past, present and future meet. She was also Triple Goddess of the Moon carrying a torch through the skies, as she did in her role of Underworld guardian and guide.

Hecate, as the wise guide and initiator of women's mysteries, may be found in the myths that describe her as the Maiden Goddess Kore/Persephone's companion in the Underworld after she was abducted by the Hades.

Carrying her torch, accompanied by dogs, and with the waning moon headdress, she is a guardian (especially of women) for shadow scrying, but is said to help all who can look beyond her aging features to her inner beauty.

Good for dark crystal and incense silent scrying, any scrying by moonlight, dark mirrors, dark water scrying, and candles and shadows to encounter ancestors and spirit guides.

Candle color: Black, dark blue

Crystal: Jet

Incense: Myrrh or mugwort

Nephthys

The ancient Egyptian twin sister and alter ego of Mother Isis and wife of Seth, god of disruption, she is often most remembered for her Underworld protective role. She stands behind Osiris as the heart of the deceased is weighed to see if he or she is worthy to go to the banks of the celestial Nile in the Milky Way.

Similar to Isis, she helped to protect and comfort the dead and was one of the four protective death goddesses.

Nephthys represented sunset, and both she and Isis rode on the solar boat at the first sunrise.

As the shadow alter ego of Isis she symbolized the darkness, silence, hidden mysteries, and what was invisible.

She is shown as a woman with a pylon, a tower surmounted by a dish on her headdress, and in her protective role she has outstretched wings.

Good for all shadow scrying, especially incense and translucent spheres, and for contacting those recently deceased, especially through crystals and dark mirrors.

Candle color: Gray

Crystal: Desert rose

Fragrance: Musk or sandalwood

Nut

The ancient Egyptian creating sky mother, Nut was mother of many of the deities, including Ra, the Sun God. In his sky boat he passed through the waters of her womb each night to be reborn through her at dawn.

Mother of the sun, moon, and all heavenly bodies and stars, she is depicted as a deep blue woman covered in stars, arched over the whole earth and above the Earth god Geb, her husband, her fingers and toes touching the earth.

There are many representations of her body covered with stars, and this image was painted on tomb lids in the hope she would grant rebirth, as Ra was reborn.

Good for outdoor scrying especially by moonlight or under the stars, for any dark crystal work, and for incense scrying outdoors.

Candle color: Blue

Crystal: Lapis lazuli

Incense: Sage or myrrh

Crystal Shadow Scrying

Once your clairvoyant image system is activated through working with clear crystals, you will find that your inner imagery system means you need less and less physical stimuli.

Some clairvoyants eventually work without any focus, but others find a tangible focus such as a dark or opaque crystal—a way of drawing to them the precise knowledge or contact from beyond needed at a particular time.

Once you are confident with clearer spheres, experiment scrying with light reflected on the surface of polished opaque balls or eggs.

Suitable crystals include patterned agate, obsidian, rainbow obsidian, translucent moonstone, and rainbow or silver moonstones.

Also effective is green mottled onyx, laboradite with iridescent rainbow shimmers, blue celestite made up of lots of tiny light blue crystals that often has pathways and holes leading within for psychic journeys to other dimensions, and amethyst geodes where tiny crystals are embedded in rock similar to a miniature cave.

Silvery white selenite or Satin Spar with a white glistening strip round or through it, as moonstone is perfect for moonlight scrying.

Try also eggs of green translucent or gleaming jade, ice-like, or polished calcite in different colors, such as soft green, blue, and honey yellow, green and black malachite, deep blue and gold lapis lazuli flecked with stars, brown gleaming tiger or red ox eye, red and green ruby in zoisite, and ocean or orbicular jasper covered with orbs of white, blue, cream, orange, and lighter green.

I have seen beautiful opaque crystal spheres with surfaces that resemble crystalline maps of the world such as maps of the world that are very good for past life recall and work with other dimensions as well as for meditation. You can buy a collection of different translucent and opaque crystals over time, varying from small ones the size of a quail's egg to a large hen's-egg size for special scrying sessions.

Online stores usually have photographs so you can see the right sphere or egg for you. If possible, visit a mineral store— they tend to be cheaper than New Age stores. At mineral stores staff are often experts in mineralogical properties, and stones tend to be of a high quality.

Beginning Shadow and Light Scrying With Crystals

Don't worry about asking and trying to answer questions at this stage, but ask the blessings of the guardian of the crystal, whom you will sense rather than see. First, spend time trying your chosen translucent and/or opaque crystals by shining candles or experimenting with sun and moonlight to study the different effects of light and shadow on the surface. One or two will become your natural scrying tools, but you may like to acquire a collection, as they are great energizers and protectors of the home or workplace.

It is easiest is to start with a very dark gleaming sphere, such as obsidian or the more shimmering rainbow obsidian, as large as you can afford. They are not expensive, but black onyx is a good substitute. Obsidian was first adopted for scrying by the Mayans and the Aztecs, who used obsidian mirrors to view eclipses (see Chapter 11).

It should be easily held in your hand as you do need to move the crystal around both for the psychometric fingertip impressions, and to catch different angles of your light source to contrast and make patterns with the shadows on the surface. Work in darkness and shine candles around the dark sphere so the light within it forms faint moving images. A slightly open window or a small fan will cause a flickering effect.

The light, whatever time of day or kind of crystal, should shine actually on the surface as light spheres or shimmers.

Selenite, moonstone, especially rainbow or silver moonstone or rose quartz, blue celestite, or amethyst geodes are best in full or bright moonlight, but do not work so well in sunlight. Opaque lighter spheres similar to the agates or ruby in zoisite are the best sunlight shadow scryers.

If you are using an opaque agate or other crystal, egg, or sphere choose one with a number of patterns, colors, shades of colors, and variations of dark and light already etched on the surface.

Shadow Crystal Scrying to Answer Questions

Translucent or opaque crystals are better for personal decision-making in any area of life rather than for advising others, as the technique is not so easily taught to a client during a clairvoyant session. Translucent crystals are good for emotional issues. Dark crystals are especially potent for revealing hidden matters and for what is unexpected, and also the more distant future.

Work in silence. If scrying after dark, often recommended as the best time for darker crystals, light six small white candles in a horseshoe around the back and sides of the crystal so the light is shining directly into the crystal egg or sphere.

Pass the sphere silently over the candle or candle flame, asking in your mind that it be cleansed and filled with light.

Similar to the scryers of Asia, who introduced the art of scrying with agates thousands of years ago, gaze at the markings on your chosen crystal egg or sphere in the light while you think of a question or a person about whom you would like to ask. Cradle the crystal and rub your hands over the surface to pick up psychometric impressions.

When you have your question in your mind, hold the egg in your left hand (if you are right-handed) and rotate it slowly clockwise nine times so you catch the light in it. As you do so, repeat your question in your mind nine times, the number of perfection.

Now hold the egg lightly between your hands, and keep turning it slowly in all directions within the light.

Some people actually see faint moving images in the light and shadow unfolding on the surface. They are similar to very old-fashioned, flickering, black-and-white films, as in mirrors, or they may be similar to impressions that become clear, fade back into the crystal, and emerge for longer and longer periods, then becoming more transient and less distinct. Then the image or picture will go and you need to start again to look for another one.

At this point, turn your egg again, this time counterclockwise nine times, and as you do this the meaning of the image or scene will come into your mind, rather than on the ball as an inner, vivid vision. It may be accompanied by words in your mind as phrases from poetry, sacred writings, or words of wisdom from your inner voice, or in the familiar soft tones voice of a Guardian Angel, Spirit Guide, or wise ancestor.

To see a second and subsequent image, repeat the question in your mind as when you first held the sphere, starting with it between your hands, then rotating it in your left hand, and finally turning it with both hands. You may find the question has changed slightly in view of the first image's information. Finish each part of the reading with the counterclockwise rotation.

Images can run though your life from past, to present, to future, but mainly suggest scenes of your own life as it could become or reveal symbols that point a way forward.

The more experienced you become with dark crystals, the less you may rely on the external images you perceive on the surface. Over time, even the faintest transient image of the surface will instantly be translated into rich inner symbols and words.

In this way you will increasingly rely on opaque and translucent crystals for inspiration and to channel wisdom from guides and ancestors, and less for specific questions.

Smoke Divination

Natural smoke divination occurs at hot springs, pools, or geysers.

Smoke divination is sometimes combined with fire divination to give extra information, as I described in the chapter on fire scrying.

You can work with the natural smoke from an outdoor fire. Campfires and bonfires are excellent sources of wood smoke. If possible, gather the wood locally. A light breeze is best. Fire smoke divination is good for answering questions, especially about matters that need a fast response or involving anticipated change. You can also get sudden insights from the smoke of a candle, especially in the seconds after it is extinguished.

However, I would recommend scrying with incense sticks for slower and more spiritual matters. Incense has been burned in ceremonies for thousands of years. It was burned as an offering to send prayers to the deities on the fragrant smoke and at the same time to receive wisdom from them, interpreted by the priesthood in the movement of the smoke.

The fragrances and sinuous movement of incense smoke as it coils upwards readily induces a light trance state, ideal for communicating with Spirit Guides and ancestors, or beloved recently deceased relatives. The burning fragrance slows the conscious mind and opens psychic channels.

Buy good-quality sticks in natural materials, as these are not only sweeter and psychically more powerful, but are not consumed too fast.

You can, if you burn them in front of a mirror or either side of a candle, get additional stimulus from the light and shadow effect (see chapters 5, 10, and 11).

As with fire divination, smoke answers your question both by the direction of the smoke and the images it invokes in the smoke patterns, clairvoyantly within your mind.

Pure and Simple Smoke Divination

If you are using just the smoke for divination, it is best in sunlight or clear outdoor light, though you can use candles or brilliant full moonlight as a backdrop and contrast to the dark smoke. Sunset and sunrise are particularly powerful times to study smoke, particularly incense. You can work indoors or outside.

If you observe the smoke before and after divination, you may notice that concentrating on an issue in your mind dramatically affects the direction the smoke curls. This is psychokinesis in action again.

Light either a Native North American sagebrush or cedar smudge, or three or four incense sticks of a woody fragrance such as pine, cedar, juniper, or sandalwood, or any floral fragrance. Set the smudge in a low, upright container or a small heatproof dish. You can buy small smudge sticks that are ideal for this purpose by mail order.

Try a braid of sweetgrass lit in a flat heatproof dish. Sweetgrass is very magical with the smoke rising against the sunset.

Alternatively, put four incense sticks in individual holders in a square formation so that all the sticks are angled to point inwards towards the same central spot, each at about 60 degrees. You can mix the fragrances.

You can alternatively use the kind of flat holder that has four holes and direct the individual incense sticks upwards vertically. Cones are not so effective. You can also burn a dish of loose granular incense on charcoal or dried broad leaved herbs, such as sagebrush, pine, or bay leaves (often used in cooking) in a heatproof bowl or abalone shell.

As you light the smudge or the incense sticks one after the other from a candle, ask a question either out loud or in your mind.

Alternatively, ask that your Spirit Guide, or a wise ancestor or beloved relative will communicate with your either in symbols or by appearing in the smoke. You can also ask to see past worlds that will be of use now. For seeing other dimensions stare through and beyond the smoke.

You can, if you wish, stand a mirror behind the incense or smudge so you get a reflection of smoke behind the actual smoke. This time, however, you would focus on images in the smoke rather than the psychic pictures revealed by the mirror.

Interpreting Smoke Patterns

The following offers a framework for working on a deeper level with smoke images, whatever the source of smoke. Some of the traditional meanings are subtly different from those in tea leaf or coffee ground reading.

Though they may seem similar to fortune-telling meanings, studying the patterns of smoke closely attunes you with its vibrations. Indeed, you may receive a great deal of inner psychic information as a result, even if you are not consciously looking for images in the smoke, but just focusing on the patterns.

- If the smoke goes directly upwards, the answer is positive, whether to act, to speak, or to make a change. Your wish will come to fruition soon.

- If the smoke turns to the left as it rises upwards, you should seek the help of others to fulfill your plans, and they may take a little longer to fulfill than you expected.

- If it rises but turns to the right, you will succeed by your own efforts, so do not be deterred by others' doubts or criticisms that may arise out of their fear of change rather than real concerns.

- If the smoke changes direction rapidly, you should try an alternative means from the planned approach to achieve your desire.

↩ If the smoke goes in different directions, you may experience conflicting demands from others in relation to the matter under question.

↩ If the smoke goes in different directions but joins higher up, there will be reconciliation and unexpected unity from people who are usually difficult.

↩ If the smoke goes in different directions after initially converging or rising in one stream, you maybe need to ask if a relationship or situation you are considering is one you wish to be permanent, or if you are staying for comfort and need rather than because you want to.

↩ A circle indicates unity and interlocking circles, committed love, or partnership. Dots or lots of tiny circles mean money is coming.

↩ Triangles are expansion, increased opportunity, and resources and fertility.

↩ Squares signify security and property.

↩ Wavy lines mean successful journeys.

↩ Smoke that rises in two or more parallel vertical lines indicates that two different parts of your life will prosper and move in harmony.

↩ If the smoke becomes very light and wispy, spiritual matters are favored.

↩ If the smoke billows as it rises then there may be confusion or secrecy.

↩ If, however, the smoke is dark but gets progressively lighter and brighter, happiness and success are assured.

↩ If the smoke entwines or forms spirals, love and relationship are expected.

≈⊃ If the smoke flows in all directions evenly, expect travel or happy news from afar.

≈⊃ Look out for initials or numbers in the smoke. Initials can refer to significant people coming into your life if you do not already know them. Numbers indicate days or weeks according to the time frame of the question. On a whole, smoke prophecies tend to be fast and refer to weeks rather than months ahead.

Beginning Shadow Scrying

You need a white or light-colored wall, and either a shelf or a flat surface so you can stand five or six white candles of differing heights and shapes at regular intervals along the shelf. You should be able to see the candles without having to lift your head upwards while either sitting or standing.

If you have any special statues of angels, power animals, or deities arrange those on the shelf so you can see their shadows against the wall when the candles are lit.

In societies such as China and Ancient Egypt, it was believed you could animate a statue either of Sekhmet, the lion-headed fire goddess; Horus the falcon-headed sky god; or Bast, the protective cat goddess, so that they protected you in their spirit form (or less positively would go out and defeat your enemies). Obviously, we are invoking the protective and benign positive aspects of any power icons. I have a number of black basalt Egyptian deities I set between the candles, including my beloved Tauret, the pregnant hippopotamus goddess of fertility and protection of the home.

Light the first candle anytime just after twilight and into its flame sprinkle a pinch of salt for purification. Light the second candle from the first and so on left to right along the row, so that the vitality of the salt is transferred to all the flames.

If you are working on developing a special gift (for example, writing or healing), you could ask that your spirit ancestor who helps you appears in the candle shadows or, if you prefer, sends you wisdom.

You can also request that "the guide who is always with me/ has drawn close to assist this stage of my life may likewise be revealed in a manner that will bring peace and joy in the shadows." If you don't want to see the Guardian in the shadows say so. There are other ways of communicating through shadow symbols or words in your mind.

Alternatively, ask that you may glimpse the world that you knew once or that can most reveal the wisdom needed on your life path. Ask whatever you most seek from the scrying as you put salt in the first flame.

You can work with a partner if you wish to explore a past world you believe you may once have shared. One of you should ask as each of you puts a pinch of salt in the first flame, "Where was it I last saw you? Walk with me through the shadows of time that we see ourselves together once more if it is right to be."

Have a slightly open window or small, relatively silent fan so the candles flicker and move, and any statues will also appear to move (a physiological way into the spiritual realms).

Breathe slowly and regularly until you begin to see the images form, and then relax and breathe normally. Accept whatever comes. Do not try to record or analyze but just experience the moment. Be patient, as it may take a few minutes to build up the images or figures of the guide from the shadows.

If working with a partner on a past world, each of you can describe aloud what you see, hear, and sense, which may at first be a very faint feature similar to a house. Keep the a dialogue going as you tune into each other's vision and gradually build up the joint world.

After what may seem to be an hour but may only be 10 or 15 minutes, the shadows will begin to blur and merge. Begin to breathe slowly and, regularly again, and when you feel back in the everyday world, sprinkle either a pinch of dried sage or salt into the last candle you lit and give thanks to your Guardians for what you learned. If working with a partner, both of you can put sage or salt in the flame, and the person who did not speak at the opening should make the farewell thanks.

End by goodbye to whoever walked with you spiritually to cut the connection and blow out the candles in reverse order of lighting in silence.

Enjoy a few moments in the darkness and then either record in your scrying journal if alone, or discuss your experiences with your partner.

Seeing Images in Smoke

You may, from the beginning, perceive smoke images as you observe the physical movement of the smoke. If not, you can gradually try to see patterns and shapes in the smoke and then build up to images. Smoke images are the most ethereal and least physical of all external clairvoyant images, and provide a bridge to inner clairvoyance.

Through half-closed eyes look at the smoke from the incense/smudge. Follow the patterns of the smoke trails. When you were a child you may have done puzzles where part of an outline was drawn and you had to fill in the rest to reveal the picture. Smoke images are similar to that, and your psyche will supply the missing shape. Allow images to form; when you sense you have seen enough images to answer your question, relax.

Still gazing at the smoke, connections between the images will flow into your mind either as a spoken message or a vivid scene on your mind.

These insights may appear visually in the smoke, in the mirror, or in your mind's vision—all stemming from the same process.

If in doubt, draw the shapes you saw in the smoke on paper and allow your hand to make them into images by psychic doodling.

You may also see a Guardian, Guide, ancestor, or relative through the smoke. If this does not work try the following technique.

Incense in Silent or Passive Scrying

This is an old technique from magic, but it does translate well into incense scrying, especially towards twilight.

Passive incense ritual scrying is good for those needs or wishes that cannot easily be answered, sometimes because an issue is complex or we are so confused we just want to hand it to some higher force and say, "Please sort it out."

It is also a way of cultivating inner stillness if you do find slower scrying methods frustrating. In the modern world, this can sometimes be a good prelude to other forms of scrying if, after all the preparations, your mind is still buzzing with unfinished tasks and mental lists to be done after the scrying.

In time, as you practice this technique every two weeks or so, you can ask not to unravel a problem, but that your Guides and ancestors or beloved relatives will appear before you through the smoke in whatever way is most appropriate. Over the weeks as you go into even deeper states of psychic awareness through this technique you will hear them speak to you quite clearly in your mind, or occasionally aloud, and you will hear their different voices. Ask nothing, for they know what you need to hear and see through the smoke.

Beginning Passive Scrying

Passive incense scrying uses two or three incense sticks lit from a single white candle. Long burning incense sticks are better than granular incense on charcoal, which needs topping up. Put them in the same upright heatproof container so the smoke rises upwards.

You could also use incense cones on a flat heatproof dish set close together. Smudge sticks or leaves that are burning steadily out of a breeze will also serve well.

You can work either in your scrying place or anywhere indoors or out where it is quiet and you can be alone. If you have a partner with whom you are in total spiritual harmony, you could work together for the same purpose using the same incense but sitting opposite each other. This is very good to spiritually unite you if you have been having relationship problems, and you may even see a shared past world that explains present difficulties. But again, ask for and expect nothing.

The incenses for this particular technique that work best are cedar, frankincense, jasmine, lavender, myrrh, rose, and sandalwood. Have a selection of the different fragrance sticks mixed in an ordinary tall container and hold your hands over the jar until you are drawn to two or three by a tingling in your fingertips. Those are the right ones for this occasion. It does not matter if you cannot identify the fragrance.

Light the candle and then the incense from the candle. Do this in silence and do not consciously formulate the purpose, but allow the smoke to ask on your behalf.

Using one of the incense sticks write in smoke in the air, "So shall all be resolved in its own time and its own way." Sit facing the incense and picture nothing. Allow words and images to float through your mind similar to clouds, but any conscious worries or forward planning that disturb you, push symbolically into the smoke with your hands, to be carried into the cosmos. Think the words, "Blessings be on all" for each concern that arises. Continue until the sticks are burned through. When the ash is cool, scatter it onto the earth. Blow out the candle if it is still burning.

This easy ritual is mentally and spiritually difficult so persevere, because our minds and psyche naturally want to direct the proceedings.

Resist any active interpretation or visualization. If anything floats by, watch it but do not try to understand its meaning.

Your Guides or ancestors may also appear without your trying to visualize them if you persevere and are patient, and you will receive rather than messages a sense of peace and being cared for.

Shadow Scrying With Candlelight

This is a technique where you observe the shadows of candles reflected against a light wall after dark, and by the shadows formed you can see moving images that trigger visions either of your Spirit Guides or wise teachers.

They are not similar to the black-and-white images you saw while mirror scrying, for these flow very slowly and seem to carry you further and further back so the wall is no longer there, and you are looking at a world of silhouettes, but where features and details are amazingly distinct.

Rather than entering the past world, you look into it but can unmistakably identify the figure that represents you as perhaps you once were.

ASpirit Guide or ancestor form may seem to grow from one for the shadows or the merging of several, but is not at all scary.

It is similar to when you were half asleep as a child and you were aware of the shadow of a family member watching you from the lighted landing. You knew it was him or her from the shadow and you felt reassured.

This is an experience that differs from person to person but will always be fulfilling.

Scrying the secrets of the future is an exciting voyage of discovery. Scrying also releases psychic and mental energies in our lives so that not only do we feel more positive, but we have more focus, determination, and confidence radiating from our aura. As a result, other people react more favorably to us without knowing why. The world becomes more hopeful, dreams more possible to attain or at least launch, difficult situations easier to turn around. For the secrets we scry are most of all our own inner treasury, as of yet untapped, potential and places to see, and adventures to pursue.

What we see in the crystal, the mirror, or the flames is no illusion but what we can become in our daily lives.

Appendix

The Deities of Fate

Ancient Egypt

The 7 Daughters of Hathor

The seven daughters of Hathor, the goddess of love, marriage, and the home, were Egyptian goddesses of fate and visited newborn children to assign their fortune. They may have once existed as a hereditary order of seven oracular priestesses at one of Hathor's temples.

Their names are **Lady of the House of Jubilation, Lady of the Stormy Sky, Lady from the Land of Silence, Lady of the Black Earth, Lady With Hair of Fire, Lady of the Sacred Land, and Lady Whose Name Flourishes Through Power.**

Their names are often used as a pre-divination protective chant, and they are signified by seven red crystals circled around a red candle or seven red cords knotted in a circle surrounding the candle.

Candle color: Red

Crystal: Red jasper or turquoise

Incense or oil: Rose or lotus

Ancient Greece

The Moirae or Moirai

Their name means the ones who apportion fate; they are three sisters, dressed in white. They oversee each individual's thread of life from start to finish, whether mortal or deity.

Clotho was the spinner of the thread of life, and she is sometimes associated with the last month of pregnancy. She decides the moment of every birth.

Lachesis, whose name means "the chooser of lots" or "good fortune," measured the thread of life with her rod and marked out key events.

Atropos or Aisa, whose name means "what is inevitable," was the cutter of the thread of life. She chose the manner and time of a person's death.

The Moirae appeared according to Greek tradition sometimes in disguise three nights after a child's birth to decide what would be his or her special gifts and determine the course of life.

Candle color: Purple

Crystal: Sodalite

Incense or oil: Cypress or honeysuckle

Ancient Rome

The Parcae

The Roman Sisters of Fate were three very old women who spun the fate of mortal destiny. Originally there was only a single goddess, **Parca**, the midwife and birth goddess who incorporated all the roles.

However, gradually they became identified as three separate goddesses, also known as Tria Fata.

Now they are called **Nona**, who spun the thread of life, **Decuma**, who assigned it to a person, and **Morta**, who cut it, ending that person's life at the appointed time.

Candle color: Very dark blue

Crystal: Amethyst

Incense and oils: Poppy/opium or myrrh

The Norse Tradition

According to Norse myth Yggdrasil the World Tree was fed by the Well of Urd, Wyrd, or Fate, in whose waters each morning the three Norns, the sisters of Fate, scryed to give guidance to the deities.

Close to the well, the three sisters lived in their cave, and in some myths they constantly carved rune staves, which they cast into the waters to determine the fate of the deities and mortals, according to cosmic laws.

The three Sisters wove a web both of the fate of the world and the fate of individual beings, mortal, and gods. They wove, not according to their own whims, but according to Orlog, the eternal law of the universe.

The first Norn, **Urdhr**, the oldest of the sisters, looked backwards and talked of the past, which in Viking tradition influenced not only a person's own present and future, but that of his or her descendants.

The second Norn, **Verdhandi**, a young, vibrant woman, looked straight ahead and talked of present deeds that also influenced the future.

Skuld, the third Norn, who tore up the web as the other two created it, was closely veiled, and her head was turned in the opposite direction from Urdhr. She held a scroll containing what would pass, given the intricate connection with past and present interactions.

The Anglo-Saxons called the Norns the Three Mothers or Modrones.

Candle color: Golden brown

Crystal: Amber

Incense or oil: Pine or sage

The Celtic Tradition

The Madronae were three goddess fate figures, each depicted as nursing a baby or with grain, fruit, symbols of fertility, and good fortune. Because the only statues or stone reliefs we have of them date from the Roman times, they are often a mixture of the Roman Matronae or Matres and the old Celtic Mothers.

They are often shown wearing long robes with one breast exposed as if to feed a child.

Candle color: Orange

Crystal: Moss agate

Incense or oil: Patchouli or rosemary

Native North America

Grandmother Spider Woman, who appears in the myths of a number of Native North American nations, is the Creatrix Fate goddess who wove the web of the world and peopled it with figures from the earth made from four different clays: red, white, yellow, and brown. Tawa or Grandfather Sun breathed life into them.

Candle color: Any natural undyed candle

Crystal: Desert rose

Incense or oil: Sagebrush or sweetgrass

Useful Reading

Agrippa, Henry Cornelius, James Freake, and Donald Tyson. *Three Books of Occult Philosophy*. St. Paul, Minn.: Llewellyn's Sourcebooks, 2002.

Andrews, Ted. *Crystal Balls and Crystal Bowls: Tools for Ancient Scrying and Modern Seership*. St. Paul, Minn.: Llewellyn Publications, 1995.

Browne, Sylvia. *Sylvia Browne's Book of Dreams*. New York: E.P. Dutton, 2002.

Buchanan-Brown, John, et. al. *The Penguin Dictionary of Symbols*. London: Penguin Books, 2004.

Buckland, Ray. *Practical Color Magic*. St Paul, Minn.: Llewellyn Publications, 1996.

Cunningham, Scott. *Complete Book of Incense, Oils and Brews*. St. Paul, Minn.: Llewellyn Publications, 2004.

———. *Encyclopedia of Crystal, Gem and Metal Magic*. St. Paul, Minn.: Llewellyn Publications, 1991.

———. *Encyclopedia of Magical Herbs*. St. Paul, Minn.: Llewellyn Publications, 1997.

Davis, Brenda. *The Seven Healing Chakras*. Berkeley, Calif.: Ulysses Press, 2000.

Davidson, Gustav. *A Dictionary of Angels.* London: Simon and Schuster, 1994.

Dee, John. *Essential Readings.* Berkley, Calif.: North Atlantic Books, 2003.

De Givry, Grillot. *Witchcraft, Magic & Alchemy.* New York: Dover Books, 1971.

Eason, Cassandra. *Art of the Pendulum.* Portland, Maine: Red Wheel/Weiser, 2004.

———. *Aura Reading.* London: Piatkus Books, 2000.

———. *Candle Power.* New York: Sterling Press, 2000.

———. *Cassandra Eason's Complete Book of Natural Magick.* Slough, UK: Quantum/Foulsham, 2004.

———. *Cassandra Eason's Book of Modern Dream Interpretation.* Slough, UK: Quantum/Foulsham, 2005.

———. *Complete Guide to Faeries and Magical Beings.* Portland, Maine: Red Wheel/Weiser, 2003.

———. *Contact your Spirit Guides.* Slough, UK: Quantum/Foulsham, 2005.

———. *The Illustrated Directory of Healing Crystals.* London: Collins and Brown, 2004.

———. *Touched by Angels.* Slough, UK: Quantum/Foulsham, 2005.

Higley, Connie, Alan Leatham, and Pat Leatham. *Aromatherapy A to Z.* Carlsbad, Calif.: Hay House, 2002.

Holland, Eileen. *Holland's Grimoire of Magical Correspondences, A Ritual Handbook.* Franklin Lakes, N.J.: New Page Books, 2005.

Hoffman, David. *Complete Illustrated Holistic Herbal.* Rockport, Mass.: Element, 1996.

Larkin, Chris. *The Book of Candlemaking: Creating Scent, Beauty and Light.* New York: Sterling, 1998.

Luciani, Vera. *Historia.* Chicago: Bolchazy-Carducci Publishers, 1991.

MacLean, Adam. *A Treatise on Angel Magic, Magnum Opus Hermetic Sourceworks.* Portland, Maine: Red Wheel/Weiser, 2006.

McArthur, Margie. *The Wisdom of the Elements, the Sacred Wheel of Earth, Air, Fire and Water*. Berkeley, Calif.: Crossing Press, 1998.

Meckaharic, Draja. *Spiritual Cleansing, a Handbook of Psychic Protection*. Portland, Maine: Red Wheel/Weiser, 2003.

Mizumoto, Sandra, and Posey Sandra. *Café Nation, Coffee Folklore, Magic and Divination*. Santa Monica, Calif.: Santa Monica Press, 2000.

Neal, Carl E. *Incense Crafting and the Use of Magickal Scents*. St. Paul, Minn.: Llewellyn Publications, 2003.

Radin, Dean. *The Conscious Universe, the Scientific Truth of Psychic Phenomena*. New York: HarperCollins, 1997.

Waite, Arthur Edward. *The Hermetical and Alchemical Writings of Paracelsus*. New York: Kessinger Publishing, 2005.

Weiss, Brian L. *Meditation, Achieving Inner Peace and Tranquility in Your Life*. New York: Hay House, 2002.

Index

Aesculapius, 154

Aether, 123

Aftiel, 244

Agni, 69

Air, scrying with, 87-106

Airmid, 108

Akashic Records, 7

Angels of twilight and
    darkness, 244-245

Apheliotes, 98

Archangels of twilight and
    darkness, 244-245

Archangels, 32-35

Aristotle, 6

Athyr, 180

Azaziel, 168

Bedouins, 115

beeswax, 121, 124-125

Bes, 160-161

Bokwus, 100

Boreas, 97

Brighid, 122

candle scrying, 77-85

candlelight,shadow scrying
    with, 261

candles for wax scrying,
    choosing, 124-126

candles, mirrors and, 177-179

Cassiel, 244

Celtic Circling Prayer, the, 31-32

chakras, 38-40

clairaudience, 9, 18-19

clairsentience, 9, 20-21

clairvoyance, 7-8, 9, 17

cloud angels, 90-92

cloud scrying, 88-97

cloud work, collective, 96-97

clouds, color and, 218-220

coffee grounds, scrying
    with, 235-241

Collective Unconscious, 7, 9

color, clouds and, 218-220

Constantine, 88

Crusades, 137

crystal balls, scrying
with, 203-220

crystal dreams, 158-159

crystal shadow scrying, 248-251

crystalline water, 63

Cururipur, 100

dark mirror scrying, 185-202

Dee, Sir John, 168, 206

deities of fate, 21, 263-266

divination, geomantic, 114

divination, scrying and, 9-10

divination, smoke, 252-256

divination, stone and
sand, 114-119

dream incubation, 153

dream scrying, 153-163

dreams, love and, 162-163

Dryads, 101

Earth scrying, 107-120

east wind, 98

Eidetic imagery, 17

Enoch, 138, 168

Enochian Magick, 206

Eternal Flame of Rome, 66

fate, deities of, 21, 263-266

Fire, scrying with, 65-85

Fortune, Dion, 11

Gabriel, 34, 91, 236

geomantic divination, 114

Ghillie Dhu, 101

Gianes, 101

Gorky, Maxin, 174

Hamadryadniks, 101

Hamadryads, 101

Hathor mirrors, 179-183

Hathor, 166-167, 179-183

healing hour, 197

Hecate, 246

herbs, scrying with, 108-114

Hestia, 66

hydromancy, 45-64

Hyldermoder, 101

Ifa, 114

India, fire divination in, 69-70

indoor water scrying, 51-53

ink scrying, 137-152

Jeduthun, 245

journal, scrying, 27-28

Judas fires, 67

Jung, Carl, 7

Kelley, Edward, 206

Kemet, 186

Lailah, 245

leaf scrying, 103-104

Leliel, 245

love divination, mirrors
and, 168-169

love, dreams and, 162-163

Lunantishess, 102

Lunantisidhe, 102

lunar calendars, 13
Magnus, Albertus, 170-171
Maxentius, 88
Medjugorje, 89
Merlin, 168
Metatron, 138
Michael, 34, 90
Mir, 89
mirrors, candles and, 177-179
mirrors, Hathor, 179-183
mirrors, love divination
    and, 168-169
mirrors, scrying with, 165-184
moon water, 60-61
moss wives, 102
Nahaliel, 47
Nemain, 102
Nemetona, 102
Nephthys, 117, 246-247
morth wind, 97-98
Notus, 98
Nut, 247
Nyd, 66
ocean scrying, 57-59
oil scrying, 137-152
oinomancy, 222
outdoor water scrying, 53-59
Paracelsus, 203
passive scrying, 259-260
Phul, 47
Pluto, 188

processing psychic
    information, 11-12
Prophesying by Dreams, 6
psychic information, processing,
    11-12
psychokinesis, 253
psychometry, 20-21
Puthoff, Harold, 8
pyromancy, 65-85
Quetzalcoatl, 187
Radande, 102
Rahab, 47
rain water, 62
Raphael, 33, 91
Raziel, 207-209
remote viewing, 8
rock sculptures, 119-120
sand divination, 114-119
Scachlil, 245
scrying journal, 27-28
scrying,
        with Air, 87-106
        with candlelight,
        shadow, 261
        with coffee grounds,
        235-241
        with crystal balls, 203-223
        with Fire, 65-85
        with herbs, 108-114
        with mirrors, 165-184
        with shadows, 243-261
        with tea leaves, 221-234

with Water, 45-64

with wax, 121-136

scrying,

candle, 77-85

cloud, 88-97

divination and, 9-10

dream, 153-163

Earth, 107-120

ink, 137-152

leaf, 103-104

ocean, 57-59

oil, 137-152

passive, 259-260

sea, 55-56

sleep, 155-159

time and, 13-14

tress, 104-106

wind, 99-106

sea scrying, 55-56

shadows, scrying with, 243-261

Shamans, 63-64

Skogara, 102

sky angels, 90-92

slack tide, 58-59

sleep scrying, 155-159

Smith, Captain John, 236

smoke divination, 252-256

snow water, 62-63

Solomon's Seal, 207-208

south wind, 98-99

St. Augustine, 46

St. Catherine IV, 46

standard time, 13

stone divination, 114-119

storm water, 61-62

Sun water, 60

symbols, scrying and, 11, 15-16

Targ, Russell, 8

tasseography, 221-241

tasseomancy, 221-241

tea leaves, scrying
        with, 221-234

Tengu, 102

Tezcatlipoca, 187-188

Thoth, 138, 145-146

Tibet, fire divination in, 69-70

time, scrying and, 13-14

tree scrying, 104-106

Trsiel, 47

Universal Web, 7

Uriel, 33

Vesta, 66

Virgin Mary, 88-89

water angels, 47

Water, scrying with, 45-64

wax, scrying with, 121-136

Well of Wisdom, 7

west wind, 99

Williamson, Cecil, 191

wind scrying, 99-106

wind water, 61-62

wind, the power of the, 97-99

wood wives, 102

Zephyrus, 99

About the Author

Cassandra was originally trained in teaching and earned an honors psychology degree while bringing up her five children, with the intention of training as an Educational Psychologist.

Cassandra has had more than 70 books published in the UK, the United States, and all over the world.

Since 1994 when Cassandra appeared on *Nib's Unsolved Mysteries*, *Paramount Sightings*, and *The Other Side* television programs in America, her work has been featured in *The National Enquirer* and *Woman's World*.

Her books have been serialized around the world in the *Daily Mirror*, the *Daily Express*, the *News of the World*, *Spirit and Destiny*, *Fate and Fortune*, *Prediction*, *Best and Bella*, *Homes and Gardens*, *Good Housekeeping*, and in *Woman's Day* and *New Ideas*. She currently writes a monthly master class for *Beyond* magazine.

She has been acknowledged as a world expert on parent/child intuitive links and has appeared many times on television and radio, including *Sky News*, *Strange but True*, *Heaven and Earth*, *Richard and Judy*, and *Sky Living's Jane Goldman Investigates*. In the UK she had her own weekly miniseries, *Sixth Sense*, on United Artists Cable network for a number of years. She acted as psychic consultant/resident expert on the successful *Magic and Mystery* series and now does occasional pieces as a psychic expert for GMTV. She has analyzed dreams on the *Big Brother* series and *Celebrity Big Brother*. Currently, she is working on a New Age CD production of psychic workshops with Paradise Music.

Cassandra has lectured at Oxford, London, and Glasgow Universities on the paranormal and was an Honorary Research Fellow at the Alister Hardy Research Centre in Oxford for three years.

Cassandra is an expert on crystals and crystal healing, folk lore, superstitions, Celtic wisdom, Wicca, fairies, sacred sites, earth energies, Druidry, maternal instinct, psychic children, scrying, survival after death, women's spirituality, divination of all kinds, and natural magic.

Cassandra teaches and runs workshops in psychic development, magic and Witchcraft, all forms of divination, crystals, healing, aura, and chakra work and nature spirituality. She is also a practicing Druidess. Online, through her extensive Website, *www.cassandraeason.co.uk*, Cassandra offers online information, advice to individuals, and online courses. She has five children and two black cats, and lives on a small rural island off the South Coast of England, the Isle of Wight.